The Evolution of Art and Architecture:

From Ancient Times to the Present Day

The Evolution of Art and Architecture: From Ancient Times to the Present Day

Authors

Austin Mardon

James Plaxton, Mehvish Masood, Jaime Johnson,
Naharah Wilmot, Sophia Kazakoff, Muhammad Farooq

Edited by

Andrei Kazakoff

Catherine Mardon

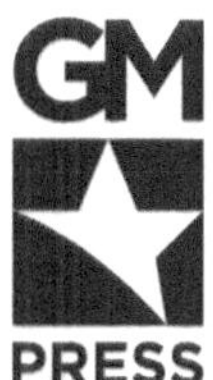

First Printing: 2023

Cover Design and typeset by Clare Dalton

Print ISBN 978-1-77889-026-0
Ebook ISBN 978-1-77889-027-7

Golden Meteorite Press
103 11919 82 St NW
Edmonton, AB T5B 2W3
www.goldenmeteoritepress.com

Contents

Introduction

Art and architecture have been integral parts of human civilizations since the beginning of time. They reflect the cultural, social, and religious values of a society and serve as a medium of communication for generations. From the grand pyramids of Egypt to the towering skyscrapers of today, the evolution of art and architecture has been a fascinating journey.

This book is an attempt to trace the history of art and architecture from ancient Greece and Rome to the modernist and postmodernist movements of the 20th century. It aims to provide a comprehensive understanding of the artistic and architectural styles that have shaped the world we live in today.

Art and Architecture in Ancient Greece and Rome

By James Plaxton

Introduction

Art and architecture in Greece and Rome have a historical significance due to the vast number of techniques and historically important contributions made. Greek art and architecture started the groundwork for styles and late the Romans adapted and diversified them (Department of Greek and Roman Art, 2022). Both art forms were based around honouring inspirational events, mythological beliefs, daily life, and even historical figures (Department of Greek and Roman Art, 2022). Though pottery, art, mosaics, and sculptures there was many art forms used by both Greeks and Romans, unfortunately many of these wonderful pieces haven't survived through the years but of what is left historians have been able to learn so much about ancient times and techniques (Art Institvte Chicago, 2022). Architecture built from this time advanced so many techniques used today, including arches, columns and even the use of concrete (Henig, 2023) (Hemingway, Architecture in Ancient Greece, 2003). It is clear that the impact of Greece and Rome had on the art and architecture advancement was significant.

Greek Art

Overview of Greek Art

Ancient Greek art had a reputation of perfectionism, the standards of a sculpture or art piece were beauty and perfection as art was idealized similar to their cultural romanticization of literary and sports (Art Institute Chicago, 2022). There were differing periods within the history around art in Greece that provided changes into the styles and techniques used, Geometric, Archaic, Classical and Hellenistic all spanning within 900 and 30 BCE (Gill, 2019).

Within the Geometric period, patterns and geometric shapes were prevalent, in addition there was significant abstract figures such as horses and miliary (Art Institute Chicago, 2022). The Archaic period, which was from 650 to 480 BCE, this period was heavily influenced from Egypt and Eastern regions (Art Institute Chicago, 2022). Terracotta cases were dominant in this art period as techniques including black and red figure decoration allowed for an increased range of creatures, plants, and daily depictions to be displayed (Art Institute Chicago, 2022). The classical period or the Golden Age of Greece, are home to many significant artistic achievements as Athens became a flourishing art destination after the defeat of the Persians in 479 BCE. The form of three-dimensional art increased in popularity (Gill, 2019). Lastly the Hellenistic period, which was from 322 though 30 BCE, this period was defined after the loss of Alexander the Great. Greek art transitioned into the honoring of Gods and heroes through large scale perfect sculptures (Art Institvte Chicago, 2022).

Depiction of Mythological Themes Used within Greek Art

The Greeks took great inspiration from mythology when it came to their art, they had characters, stories and general themes that were then communicated though art form in a way of honouring their historical and cultural values and beliefs (Hemingway, 2003). Many myths, characters and legends have been discovered by the modern world due to the detailed forms of art the Greeks had (History.com Editors, 2009).

Throughout the art recovered from ancient Greece there has been myths that are predominant and well established these include Hercules, Trojan War, Odysseus, Titanomachy, and the underworld (Hemingway, 2003). Hercules was a dominant mythological theme within Greek art, the story of the twelve labours of Hercules was seemingly treasured in that time (History.com Editors, 2009). The Trojan War was significant to the people of Greece, historically this event was a ten year long siege or blockade of the city of Troy which led to a long-anticipated victory by the Greece forces (Hemingway, 2003). Following the defeat of Troy, the story of Odysseus began with his ten-year journey home, many art forms were utilized to chronicle this tale (Hemingway, 2003). The Titanomachy was a major myth that the Greeks loved to portray through art, this was a ten year long war between the Olympian Gods and the Titans (Hemingway, 2003). Lastly the underworld provided a plethora of sources for Greek artists to base decisions off of, things such as dead souls, tales of gods, and many more elements of the underworld was extremely dominant in all art forms (History.com Editors, 2009). These are just a few examples of the mythological tales and themes that were a leading source or muse for ancient Greek art.

Artistic Forms of Expression

Sculptures that came from Ancient Greece are some of the most influential pieces in all of history, thankfully we still do have a far collection of sculptures from these time period and specific artists (Gill, 2019). Some of the most popular and historically important sculptors from Greece were Lysippus, Myron, Praxiteles, Scopas, Phidias, and Polyclitus (Gill, 2019). Specific examples of noteworthy sculptures from this Greece within this time frame include the Parthenon Marbles, The

Laocoön Group, Winged Victory of Samothrace, The Apollon Dephi, and Doryphoros (Adhikari, 2022). While there are many more examples of influential sculptures from this time period there are some the more popular and significant historically. These artists and pieces served as a strong influence in future art including the Renaissance and later in the modern era (Art Institute Chicago, 2022).

Historical records show that the Greeks did enjoy painting and that it was a significant form of art for them, unfortunately there are very few painting that have survived (Art in Context, 2022).

In contract one form of art that did survive through the years was the pieces done on pottery or ceramics. Many of these pieces show the level of detail and precision the Greeks had when painting (Art in Context, 2022). Ancient Greeks used pottery to express themselves and for various practical uses, some examples being functional (bowl, pitchers, etc.) and decorative purposes. All of these pieces were of the highest quality with ranging styles to reflect various elements including cultural and political, mythological themes and story telling and of course to reflect the creative and current artistic style and techniques as well (Art in Context, 2022). Scholars have been able to learn and analysis pottery to uncover historical events and valuable information about this time period (Art in Context, 2022).

Ancient Greece had many amazing artists who created amazing and historically important pottery pieces from all the differing in styles including red and black figure pottery in regard to how it was decorated, and amphorae, and kylix specific to the shape of which the pottery was formed (Department of Greek and Roman Art, 2022). Black figure pottery was a very popular technique used by painting black figures on a red background, it was used significantly within 600 to 500 BCE (Department of Greek and Roman Art, 2022). Red-figure pottery was a technique that developed from the prior popular black-figure pottery style and was just reversed therefore the background is black and the figures are in red (Department of Greek and Roman Art, 2022). Artists found that this allowed for more natural portrayed in and higher quality of intricate detailing, this reverse style allowed for a significant advancement in the Greek pottery world (Art in Context, 2022). Amphorae was a shape of pottery that was significantly popular within Ancient Greece at the time. It was a large jug with two handles on the side that had both functional uses such as transportation and storage of oils, wines, grains: however, were also used as a decorative piece (Barrientos, 2020). These types of potteries were known for their captivating artwork that featured historical event, mythology and led to a further understanding of ancient Greek culture (Barrientos, 2020). The other shape or style of pottery that was popular at the time was called Kylix; this was a stemmed cup that was shallow in nature. These pottery pieces were typically used for drinking wine and again were decorated in either red or black figure techniques (Art Institvte Chicago, 2022).

Roman Art

While the Romans were heavily influenced by Greek art, there were other civilizations that also influenced their artistic style, including ancient Egyptians, Germans. Celtics, as well as eastern art as a whole (Art Institvte Chicago, 2023).

There are four specific periods that Ancient Roman art can be identified as based on time period, inspirations, techniques, and artists. These periods were known as the Early Roman, Republican, Imperial, and Late Antique art periods (Gill, Periods of History in Ancient Rome, 2019). The Early Roman art period was the key development of art for them and most of their inspirations from techniques to styles came from the Greeks. The most popular pieced created during this time from the Romans were sculptures, statues, and frescoes (Art Institvte Chicago, 2023). The Republican art period was when the Romans started to differentiate themselves from the Greeks and moved towards styles of realism with a main focus on intricacy and detail. While the Roman artists did continue to make last sculptures and frescoes the utilization of mosaic floors became predominate (Gill, Periods of History in Ancient Rome, 2019). Imperial art was the next period of the Roman art era following the advancement of the Roman Empire. The artists focused on creating large and grand pieces that would carry historical importance. Works including the Colum to Trajan, Bath of Caracalla, and the Arch of Titus show how monumental this art period was for the Romans (Art Institvte Chicago, 2023). Lastly the Late Antique period during this time the once strong Roman Empire was deteriorating and there was a decreased use of quality materials and innovation (Art Institvte Chicago, 2023). There are still artists who produced significate works of art including mosaics and illuminated manuscripts (Gill, Periods of History in Ancient Rome, 2019).

The Romans were incredibly passionate about sculptures, and it played an important role within daily life in Rome. Sculptures could be full body or come as just the bust meaning that it was only the subject's head (Art Institvte Chicago, 2023). The sculptures could also come as a "relief" which meant it was directly part of the wall, and lastly though sarcophagi which were sculptures of tombs (Art Institvte Chicago, 2023). The Romans use sculptures to decorate public spaces, buildings, as well as private homes and gardens. Due to the heavy influence of Ancient Greek on the Roman sculpture's techniques, the Romans actually created copies of Greek sculptures to have within their homes and on display which a majority being commissioned for wealthy Romans (Art Institvte Chicago, 2023). Similar to the Greek inspirations, Romans based sculptures off of philosophers, gods and goddesses, famous athletes as well as historically important people or figure heads (Gill, Periods of History in Ancient Rome, 2019).

Busts were a significant part of ancient Rome and their art style, as this wasn't something that was as popular for Greek artists it was a way that

Roman artists were able to diversify themselves (Art Institvte Chicago, 2023). The sculpture would be just of the head sometimes of wealthy Romans who wanted a shrine to themselves or of their ancestors to honor the lineage (Art Institvte Chicago, 2023). There are a significant number of famous busts that still remained today an have been utilized to honor a significant amount of philosophers throughout Roman museums and historical homes (Henig, 2023).

Romans also used painting as an art form, using mostly frescoes, which were art pieces painted directly on the walls of homes and buildings (Art Institvte Chicago, 2023). Unfortunately, majority of these art pieces were destroyed overtime, however, there are some still preserved within the city of Pompeii After everything was preserved from the volcanic eruption (Gill, Periods of History in Ancient Rome, 2019).

Greek Architecture

In 450 B.C. the Athenians started to build grand displays of architecture after increased funding from the general Pericles (Art Institvte Chicago, 2022). The general thought that by allocating dues from allies to these grand displays of building would first bring people into the city but also provide work for the locals (Art Institvte Chicago, 2022).

Long horizontal columns, elaborate details, symmetrical and balanced in nature were the key characteristics of Greek architecture which has been replicated by monuments and government buildings globally (Hemingway, Architecture in Ancient Greece, 2003). There is a real variety of buildings that the Greeks were known for however some of these unfortunately didn't survive through the years, the building to survive were primarily the large-scale temples that were built to honour and worship their gods (Hemingway, Greek Gods and Religious Practices, 2003).

There are six key elements of Greek architecture that can be characterized as columns, pediments, entablature, symmetry, materials used (primarily marble, limestone, and also clay) and openings such as windows and doors (Art Institvte Chicago, 2022). There are three styles of columns that the Greeks dominantly used: Ionic, Doric, and Corinthian (Craven, 2019). These styles could also be referred to as "orders" to reflect the specifics of column used. Most columns had long horizontal grooves that were referred to as fluting regardless or the style or "orders" used, these fluting details accentuated the depth of the columns and helped create a stronger illusion of symmetry (Craven, 2019). Ionic styled columns were thin with a wide base, they typically had detailing at the top in the form of scrolls or other various designs (Hemingway, Architecture in Ancient Greece, 2003). In contract to the Ionic style the Doric style was more simplistic no designs, and were relatively wider or thicker, they did narrow at the top similar to the Ionic (Craven, 2019). The last style that was predominant in Greek architecture was called Corinthian, this style was the more intricate or decorative of the three detailed with scrolls, leaves of plants and other relevant designs (Craven, 2019). This style was heavily duplicated by the Romans in their future architecture. A pediment was the triangle section of the building between the roof and was typically housing significant sculptures (Craven, 2019). Entablatures were the portion of a building that rests between the columns and roof and was structurally important to supporting the roof (Craven, 2019). There were three distinct elements to an entablature being the architrave, frieze, and lastly the cornice (Craven, 2019).

Temples were a large element of Greek architecture being grand in nature and had a relatively simplistic design (Hemingway, Architecture in Ancient Greece, 2003). Typically, the exterior of the building was encased with columns featuring various styles as previously earlier (Hemingway, Architecture in Ancient Greece, 2003). Typically, inside the temple there was a chamber at which the God or goddess's statue would be on display or protected. One of the most famous temples from ancient Greece is called the Parthenon, which is located within the city of Athens (Hemingway, Architecture in Ancient Greece, 2003). It was built in honor of Athena out of gold and ivory and featured styles of the Doric column, specifically having over forty-six outer columns at thirty-four feet tall (Hemingway, Architecture in Ancient Greece, 2003).

In addition to temples, the Greeks were known for many public buildings and structures. For example, theatres that hosted seating for large masses, typically built into the side of a hill which allowed for optimal acoustics as sound travelled up (Craven, 2019). They also built structures called "Stoas", this was a structure used by merchants to sell goods or others to host meetings under covered walkways (Hemingway, Architecture in Ancient Greece, 2003).

Roman Architecture

Roman architecture stems from ancient Greek architecture as the romans used similar techniques and styles regardless of their similarities, there are some distinct features that characterize Roman architecture solely. Arches are one of the main characteristics of Roman architecture since they invented the arch, it allowed for larger more complex structures such as bridges, aqueducts, and other large public buildings (Henig, 2023). Sometimes arches were left to be simple and undecorated, but majority of the time they had intricate carvings featured on them (Gill, Periods of History in Ancient Rome, 2019). Vaults for another element of roman architecture developed by Roman architects and utilized heavily (Art in Context, 2021). Vaults are a continuous series of arches, it was one way that Roman architects were able to create long, functional spaces that were impressive visually (Art in Context, 2021). Roman architects were also of the more creative when it came to the materials they used within their structures (Henig, 2023). They were ones to experiment and mastered the use of concrete (Henig, 2023). Concrete allowed Roman architects to build various components, designs and shapes that were untraditional and unique for the time (Henig, 2023).

Roman architects also use domes within their building styles, this was inspired from Greek architecture, however, due to their materials and use of arches they were able to create significantly larger domes, such as the Patheon in Rome (Ranogajec, 2015). The Romans were able to create visually appealing, yet functional large spaces by utilizing domes (Henig, 2023). One of the most significant architectural builds from ancient Rome is the Colosseum built in 1st century AD (Henig, 2023). The Colosseum served as an amphitheatre which could allow for around fifty-thousand guests, and it was the site of the early Olympic or gladiator games, public events, and much more (Gill, Periods of History in Ancient Rome, 2019).

The ancient Romans had many architectural buildings of importance and did place significant emphasis on public buildings, including temples, boat houses, basilicas, and public squares (Henig, 2023). These buildings were used as a source of public appeal, dominance, as well as an outlet for artists to express their talents as many of these public buildings featured mosaics, frescoes, and various other forms of Roman art created from this time (Art Institvte Chicago, 2023).

Conclusion

From timeless works of pottery telling the stories of ancient Greece, grand mosaics from ancient Rome, even the Colosseum and Patheon all of these works of art and architecture are extremely historically significant. Various outstanding techniques were developed allowing for future advancement of art for pottery, paintings and sculptures and skill when constructing buildings and structures. Even today artists and architects refer to the basics that were developed from Greece and Rome when making new developments in their field. Just as the Romans used and developed skills from the Greeks, these techniques are still being used and improved in present day (Henig, 2023).

References

Adhikari, S. (2022, November 14). Top 12 Ancient Greek Sculptures. Retrieved from Ancient History Lists: https://www.ancienthistorylists.com/greek-history/top-ancient-greek-sculptures/

Art in Context. (2021, October 20). Roman Architecture – An Inside Look at Ancient Roman Buildings. Retrieved from Art in Context: https://artincontext.org/roman-architecture/

Art in Context. (2022, June 9). Greek Paintings – An Exploration of the Best Ancient Greek Paintings. Retrieved from Art in Context: https://artincontext.org/greek-paintings/

Art in Context. (2022, March 12). Greek Pottery – An Overview of the Development of Ancient Greek Pottery. Retrieved from Art in Context : https://artincontext.org/greek-pottery/

Art Institvte Chicago. (2022). ANCIENT GREEK. Retrieved from Art Institvte Chicago: https://www.artic.edu/artists/2601/ancient-greek

Art Institvte Chicago. (2023). ANCIENT ROMAN ART. Retrieved from Art Institvte Chicago: https://www.artic.edu/highlights/19/ancient-roman-art

Barrientos, A. (2020, July 21). Ancient Art of Amphora Pottery. Retrieved from Classical Wisdom: https://classicalwisdom.com/art/ancient-art-of-amphora-pottery/

Brenner, C. (1996). The Inquiring Eye: Classical Mythology in Eastern Europe.

Craven, J. (2019, June 2). The Entablature Helps You Get That Greek Revival Look. Retrieved from Thought Co. : https://www.thoughtco.com/what-is-an-entablature-3953692

Department of Greek and Roman Art. (2022, October). Athenian Vase Painting: Black- and Red-Figure Techniques. Retrieved from The Metropolitan Museum of Art: https://www.metmuseum.org/toah/hd/vase/hd_vase.htm

Gill, N. (2019, July 8). Famous Ancient Greek Sculptors. Retrieved from Thought Co: https://www.thoughtco.com/6-ancient-greek-sculptors-116915#:~:text=These%20six%20sculptors%20(Myron%2C%20Phidias,in%20Roman%20and%20later%20copies.

Gill, N. (2019). Periods of History in Ancient Rome. Retrieved from Thought Co.: https://www.thoughtco.com/periods-of-history-in-ancient-rome-120845

Hemingway, C. (2003, October). Architecture in Ancient Greece. Retrieved from The Metropolitan Museum of Art: https://www.metmuseum.org/toah/hd/grarc/hd_grarc.htm

Hemingway, C. (2003, October). Greek Gods and Religious Practices. Retrieved from The Metropolitan Museum of Art: https://www.metmuseum.org/toah/hd/grlg/hd_grlg.htm

Henig, M. (2023). Roman Art and Architecture. Retrieved from Oxford Art Online: https://www.oxfordartonline.com/page/roman-art-and-architecture?t:state:client=6CpQjI3WVaBG0sY+535+-jLaz/cw=:H4sIAAAAAAAAAFWOvUoDQRSFb/xBJdjY+AK2mR/dmA2WoiFkESFof9m9riOzM+PMZWMaW0tfxBeytrazsnJsBIsD5/AdDuftE7ZXWwAwSBEWPrYCA9b3JBgDJY7rsTCOKTq0IlHsTU-1JnFtDjq8

History.com Editors. (2009, December 2). Greek Mythology. Retrieved from HISTORY: https://www.history.com/topics/ancient-greece/greek-mythology

Ranogajec, P. (2015, December 11). The Pantheon (Rome). Retrieved from Smart History: https://smarthistory.org/the-pantheon/

Egyptian Art and Architecture

By Mehvish Masood

The civilization of Ancient Egypt is one that survived for thousands of years and is thought to be a highly-developed society with its own customs and practices. Looking into the art and architecture of this time gives great insight into the lifestyle and practices of people within this society. Notably, not much is left from this civilization due to a lack of preservation. Much of the analysis that can occur are on items from tombs and funerary processions, as these are the things that have remained until now. Nonetheless, to give an introduction into the art and architecture of this time, this article will go through the Egyptian origin story, artistic elements, terminology, and themes. Then, three famous examples of art/architecture will be described.

Egyptian Origin Story

Many artistic art and architecture played a cultic purpose in terms of worshiping the gods and connecting to them in different ways. So, understanding the different gods and the story of creation does play an important role in understanding Egyptian art. The creation story goes like this. Within the very beginning, prior to the creation of the world, there was Nun, otherwise known as chaos and waters. One day, out of the waters and standing on a mound came the creator or what can be considered as "god." Who this creator was depended on the time period in question and the views in question. Nonetheless, this creator god gave birth to Shu and Tefnut, which were air and ether respectively (Robins,

2008). Then, Shu and Ternut went and had children: Geb and Nut, Earth and Sky respectively. These children notably formed the boundaries under which Shu and Tefnut, their parents, lived within. Following this, Geb and Nut had four children: Nephthys, Seth, Isis, Osiris. This is where it becomes a bit more complicated. So, after the four children were born, Osiris ruled over the world with his wife, Isis (Robins, 2008). Unfortunately, Seth killed Osiris due to jealousy and then took over the world. What Seth did not account for was the power of Isis and Nephthys as through their combined power they were able to bring Osiris back. This chain of events, however, did have repercussions for Osiris because he could not no longer be king of the living anymore. So, in response, he became the king of the dead. However, there was some level of justice because Osiris' death was avenged by his son, Horus. Seth was overthrown by Horus, who then took over the land of living for himself (Robins, 2008).

This origin story is especially important because kings were viewed as gods and much of their legitimacy came from this fact (Robins, 2008). As in, kings were thought to "hold" the spirit of Horus within them. As the king died, the spirit of Horus moved to the successor. This way of making a connection between the king and god allowed for dualism of having a living body and stil being in contact with elements of the dead. Furthermore, having the spirit of the gods within him meant that the king was the main mediator between the gods and the people. His job predominantly involved keeping gods happy to ensure that the gods would help maintain the order of the created world (Robins, 2008).

Artistic Terminology

There are different terminologies of Egyptian art that need to be understood when looking at art to get a comprehensive view or understanding of what is going on. This section will describe some of the basic terminology to help with such understanding. First of all, registers are the zones and groundlines are the lines in an image (Robins, 2008). Next, notions of scale need to be understood in the sense that the scale of the different images are not meant to be proportional, but instead are meant to specify importance of different elements within the image. Generally speaking the largest image or human on a piece of art is the thing of greatest importance and smaller images are of lesser importance, even though they do sumbolize different elements (Robins, 2008). Moreover, reliefs are another piece of terminology to be understood. Reliefs generally speak to carvings on a two dimensional flat surface. There are generally two types of reliefs. A sunken relief is one where the figures are sculpted into the image and a raised relief is one where the background is carved into the image, with the figures popping out. Sunken reliefs tend to be put on the outside of images because the sun allows for details of the sculpture to be captured, while raised reliefs are preferable for the inside of buildings (Robins, 2008). Lastly, the concepts of frontality will be explored. Frontality can be described as the artistic element of making objects directly face the individual viewing the piece of art. Notably, frontality was not arbitrary but did perform a cultic purpose. If you were able to face the sculpture, then you are more likely to receive spirits from the dead if present (Robins, 2008).

Common Artistic Elements

To understand Egyptian art, there needs to be a delineation of the different key aspects that define Egyptian art and the role it played within society. Firstly, it is important to understand that Egyptian art is not necessarily "art" in the traditional sense. In current times, "art" is thought to be as items or objects that are meant to be aesthetically pleasing. However, Egyptians did not view "art" in that way. Instead, "art" was defined by the functionality of the item. Two statues may have different astethics, but if they had the same functionality, then they had the same value within this culture (Robins, 2008). Consequently, visual culture as opposed to "art" is probably better terminology to be used in reference to Egyptian art. Notably, this does suggest that functionality played an essential role for these monuments and items. For clarity, functionality refers to how all artist elements were meant to serve a purpose. For instance, a coffin was used to physically protect the body and had spells on it to protect the body (Robins, 2008).

Another element of Egyptian art concerns the notion of perspective. The informational elements of art were much more important to artists as opposed to showing a realistic perspective of the image (Robins, 2008). For this reason, perspective on art was often manipulated to show different elements within the scene. For instance, a fruit bowl would not be shown as a bowl with fruits stacked on top of each other. Instead, it would be depicted as the fruits all lined up separately in clear view so that you could see each individual fruit in isolation with the details that defined the object (Robins, 2008).

The last element that is common within Egyptian art is the composite human form (Robins, 2008). This refers to the way that humans, but mostly powerful individuals such as kings, were depicted. It is important to note that this image was not meant to be realistic. Instead, it is meant to show the human form at the most powerful. The composite involved the head shown in profile with a full view of the eye and eyebrows. The nipple and breast tended to be drawn in profile, with items on the chest such as necklaces in full view. The shoulders were shown in full view but the legs, waist, and butt were in profile. Both the feet were shown as identical with a big toe and an arch. So, overall, the image that is created is a combination of different profile and frontal views to be able to make a powerful image of the recognized individual (Robins, 2008).

Recurring Themes

Egyptian art and architecture tend to present recurring themes that come up constantly and knowing them will help understand many pieces better (Robins, 2008). First, order and chaos is a common theme that comes up with many art pieces. This theme tends to depict the Egyptian population as orderly and the outside world as chaotic. For instance, there have been hunter scenes showing the army in an ordered manner and the opposing forces as chaotic through a clustered less of lines (Robins, 2008). The next theme that comes up a lot is realism and idealism. Depending on the king, some monarchs liked being depicted as what they actually look, while others wanted to be depicted as an idealized version of themselves (Robins, 2008). Another theme or idea that comes up a lot is the idea of usupration. It was common for kings to take objects from previous kings for themselves. However, this was not viewed as a negative thing, unlike now. Instead, this was viewed as a continuation of the sharing of the Horus spirit between kings, as mentioned before (Robins, 2008). As in, all the kings were connected by the spirit of Horus so they were essentially taking things from themselves. Notably, due to this tradition, kings would often replace the names of previous kings on objects and put their own names on due to this reason (Robins, 2008). The last theme that is an essneitaly part of Egyptian art is the idea of archaism and continuity. Archaism was often used as a way to legitimize new kings. It was essentially more recent kings emulating the practives of kings to remind people of better times and to associate themselves with these figures (Robins, 2008). On the other hand, continuity refers to the idea that specific images or scenes will be recreated continuously throughout the entirety of Egyptian art. For instance, the simiting pose is one that has been seen and used across many kingships as an image of power (Robins, 2008).

Hierakonpolis Tomb 100

This tomb was found and had a highly significant painting, which has played a central role in understanding the Predynastic Egyptian Period (4,500-3,000 BCE). This plays a big role for analysis because it is the only painting found from this time. The tomb is currently thought to belong to one of the Hierakonpolis elite members, even though some individuals do hypothesize that this tomb belonged to an unknown king from that time (Leeman, 2019). Although some items were thought to have been looted a few years prior to the discovery of it, there were some items found within the tomb. Specifically, different types of vases, pots, bowls, and jars were found. Interestingly, with the exception of a few bone fragments, no trace of a body was found within the tomb (Leeman, 2019).

While tombs have been found before and after the excavation of Hierakonopolis Tomb 100, this tomb is one of great interest and significance because it contains the earliest known attempts of mural paintings within Egyptian history (Leeman, 2019). This is thought to be the beginning of the tradition of tomb decoration, a long-standing tradition present within almost all Egyptian periods of time. For this reason, studying the scenes present within the murals gives a deeper understanding into the people from that time and how they influenced future Egyptian art (Leeman, 2019).

The mural has several symbolic scenes present on it, some of which have repeated throughout Egyptian art (Leeman, 2019). For instance, the mural has several hunting or herding scenes present on it. This was presented in several different ways. For instance, there is a representation of a man appearing to lasso an antelope with a throwing stick. Alternatively, there are several animals, appearing as goats or sheep, that have been caught in a circular animal trap. There is also a man with outstretched hands that appears to be herding a group of onyx

(Leeman, 2019). Outside of these scenes, there are several ritualistic scenes. For example, there is a scene of a man holding a stick-like object above his head, above what appears to be three kneeling prisoners. Coined as a "smiting the enemy scene," similar imagery has appeared on objects like the Narmer Palette and the Ivory Label of Den (Leeman, 2019). There is also the "Master of Animals"' scene, Thought to be influenced through Mesopotamian iconography, this scene presents a central figure standing between two animals of power, thereby depicteing how that figure can control such creatures (Leeman, 2019).

The mural also had six boats present on it (Leeman, 2019). Five were shown to be similar in shape and form: boomerang-appearing objects with objects such as cabins present on top of them. These boats are thought to resemble boats of the Naqada II tribe, an influential group that is thought to have been present around the time Egypt was first made (Leeman, 2019). Nevertheless, out of the six ships, there is one ship that stood out amongst the rest of them. This ship has a high prow and is shaded in completely with black, unlike the other ships that only have the outline of a ship with no shading. It is thought that this boat is one of the elites or an individual of importance within the ancient society of the time. Regardless, overall, this mural and all the elements on it, including this ship, has been an object of great interest and has helped with informing the understanding of Egyptian civilizations for a significant period of time (Leeman, 2019).

Narmer Palette

Narmer is considered to be one of the main founders of ancient Egypt and is thought to be one of the "kings" or "pharoahs" of the first Egyptian dynasty (Toby, 2000). Notably, this time in history was thought to be significant because Egypt was created by uniting the upper and lower regions and the palette is thought to show a representation of this idea (Suelzle, 2006).

The Palette today has been preserved in such a way that both front and back sides, which have been carved in low relief, can be analyzed (Suelzle, 2006). The front has three registers, while the back has four. Both sides have a symbol called a serekh on the top register. A serekh was a symbol with elements that represented and named the Pharoah in power within it (Suelzle, 2006). The serekh on the Narmer Palette had hiroplyphs that indicated the Horus-name of Narmer. On both sides of these serekhs, are female human heads with cow horns and ears, which are either thought to be the goddess Hathor or the goddess Bat (Suelzle, 2006).

The most extensive and large image on the whole Narmer Palette is a figure of Narmer himself on the second register on the front of the palette (Suelzle, 2006). Being the largest image of the register and entire Palette is an indication of his importance. In this register, he is wearing a symbol of Upper Egypt, the image of the White crown (Suelzle, 2006). On this register, there is also a kneeling bearded component, which is thought to signify a defeated opponent from the unficiation of Egypt; a small figure of a male attendant; and a falcon that simultaneously represents the sky god and earthly manifestation of Horus (Suelzle, 2006). The third register has two naked males that appear to be fleeing from the scene or possibly are dead. Notheless, this side of the Palette presents strong evidence of Narmer, an Upper Egypt individual, defeating the Lower Egypt polity to then unify upper and lower Egyp (Suelzle, 2006).

The Great Egyptian Pyramids of Giza

One of the most famous architectural monuments, now named as an UNESCO World Heritage Site, are the Pyramids located in Giza (Encyclopædia Britannica, n.d.). This location encompasses three separate pyramids that were built as tombs for three separate pharoahs that from the 4th Egyptian pharoah dynasty: Khufu, Kafre, and

Menkaure. They are located on a rocky plateau on the west bank of the Nile River within northern Egypt (Encyclopædia Britannica, n.d.). Notably, these are not the only pyramids to have been built by Egyptian pharoahs. However, they were by far the largest and most elaborate ones to be preserved to the present day. Furthermore, the way the pyramids currently appear is not the actual appearance when they were first made (Encyclopædia Britannica, n.d.). The pyramids actually had a limestone covering all of them, which would have made the height of the pyramids higher and the sun would have made these great monuments sparkle. However, grave robbers have almost entirely removed these encasings with the exception of one pyramid, which retains an outer limestone encasing on the topmost region (Encyclopædia Britannica, n.d.).

A question that still puzzles many is how these pyramids, which are absolutely massive monuments, were built (Encyclopædia Britannica, n.d.). Theories have been proposed, but none have been confirmed with certainty. What is considered to be the most plausible theory is that a sloping and encircling embankment, which increased in length and height as the pyramid rose, was used to haul different building equipment up the pyramid (Encyclopædia Britannica, n.d.). There are different ideas of how many workers were necessary for the building. Some think it required 100,000 men but recent evidence suggests that around 20,000 workers could have been sufficient to create these structures (Encyclopædia Britannica, n.d.). Nonetheless, these three pyramids are thought to be something of great awe from around the world and shows how advanced some of Egyptian building practices were at that time.

Conclusion

The architecture and art created by ancient Egyptians is absolutely fascinating. Studying these pieces gives a greater insight into the culture and lifestyle of individuals during the time of this great civilization.

This chapter went through some important components of Egyptian art including terminology, artistic elements, and recurring themes. Furthermore, three famous art pieces/monuments from the Egyptian world that have been preserved until now were described. The mural from Hierakonpolis Tomb 100 was described, which is one of the earliest found tomb drawings from that time. Furthermore, the Narmer Palette, which is an art-work from one of the earliest rulers of Egypt, was discussed. Lastly, some information about the pyramids of Giza, structures that are currently well-known worldwide, was provided. Notably, these are only some of the many pieces of Egyptian artwork and architecture to exist. As mentioned previously, looking into these pieces of art is essential to have an insight into this ancient civilization and get an understanding of how they influenced the world.

References

Encyclopædia Britannica. (n.d.). Pyramids of Giza. Retrieved February 27, 2023, from https://www.britannica.com/topic/Pyramids-of-Giza
Leeman, D. (2019). Tomb 100 -The Painted Tomb of Hierakonpolis. Self-Published.

Robins, G. (2008). The Art of Ancient Egypt, Revised Edition. Harvard University Press.

Suelzle, B. P. (2006). An Evaluation of Two Recent Theories Concerning the Narmer Palette. Eras, 8, 1-19.

Toby A. H. Wilkinson. (2000). What a King Is This: Narmer and the Concept of the Ruler. The Journal of Egyptian Archaeology, 86, 23–32. https://doi.org/10.2307/3822303

Wengrow, D. (2001). Rethinking ‘cattle cults’ in early Egypt: Towards a prehistoric perspective on the Narmer Palette. Cambridge Archaeological Journal, 11(1), 91-104.

The Gothic Era in Art and Architecture

By Jaime Johnson

Introduction

The Gothic Era in both art and architecture covers the 12th to the 16th centuries. This style was not a favorite among Renaissance art critics because it drastically deviated from the classic Greek and Roman styles that preceded it. However, as evidenced by movements that followed centuries after the Gothic Era, we saw a resurgence of the styles, motifs, and features that were so unique this period in architecture. This chapter captures the roots of the word Gothic, explains the inspirations that informed its distinctive architectural aesthetic, and outlines and discusses the various styles and features of the era's art and architecture that are characteristically Gothic. In this chapter, no attempts were made in terms of distinguishing art and architecture as separate disciplines because the architecture of this era was fundamentally considered art. Specific discussions of art are under the proceeding categories of architecture because the artworks are often found within the architectural structures, or they are part of its construction. For example, stained glass windows are integral to a cathedral's architectural design, but on their own can be classified as art. Other artworks discussed in the following pages such as sculptures, paintings, and illuminated manuscripts were used in conjunction with architecture as a means of decorating Gothic churches.

Why is it called Gothic?

The term Goth originates over an entire millennium before it was used to describe an era of art and architecture and it had nothing to do with artistic applications or building design. The Roman Empire ruled and controlled Europe for centuries before the Common Era, and their eventual collapse is credited to a group referred to as the Goths. The Goths were described in history as a "Germanic tribe" (Mark, n.p.). Mark (2014) notes that because scholars have argued their origins and migration, it must be concluded that they were a group of unknown descent. What cannot be argued is that they challenged Christianity and rose against Roman religious influence through invasions into Roman territories. They ultimately defeated the Romans and ushered in a new era of western civilization around the sixth century CE. The Romans considered the Goths to be "barbarians" because of their resistance to their influences and differing lifestyle.

The term Gothic was first applied to art and architecture by Giorgio Vasari (1511-1574). Vasari was an art historian, biographer of Renaissance artists, and both an artist and architect himself. His talents for architecture were appreciated more than his paintings and he was especially known for his book Lives of the Most Eminent Painters, Sculptors, and Architects, published in 1550 (Britannica, 2022). It was this book where his use of the word Gothic as an adjective for the architecture of that era was first used and it was not meant as a compliment. He compared the artists and architects of that time to the Goths, describing them and their work as barbaric and even monstrous (Chapuis, 2002) (The Art Story, n.d.). The word Gothic continued to hold a negative meaning until the Gothic Revival in the 18th century when the style resurfaced in England. It continued to be an influence on architecture and was seen more positively into the 19th and 20th centuries (The Art Story, n.d.), and even spawned a new genre of literature in the process, Gothic fiction.

Origins of Gothic Architecture

Named as the original Gothic structure, the Basilica of Saint Denis finished construction in 1144, and is located just north of Paris, France. Suger, (1081-1151) was responsible for its construction and thus, the innovative architectural features that qualifies this church as the prime example of Gothic architecture (Sack, 2022), even though he was not an architect. Suger was an abbot and an advisor to King Louis VI and VII, (Rockwell, 2023). The Basilica of Saint Denis served as the final resting place for French monarchs and Suger became abbot of the church in 1127. By 1137, it was decided that the church would be rebuilt as it was in a great state of decay (Sack, 2022). Suger's ideas for the renovation were inspired by the writings of Dionysius of Areopagite, who suggested that light would allow one to be closer to God because it was associated with divinity (Ashworth, 2022). Dr. Beth Harris notes that Suger was under the impression he was reading the writings of Saint Denis, the patron Saint of France (Smarthistory, 2020). Suger's reconstructions were to the western and eastern ends of the church. To accommodate large masses and to let in more light, Suger had three entrances built on the western façade in the style of the Roman Arch of Constantine. On the eastern side of the building, Suger constructed an ambulatory, which was a pathway that led patrons around and behind the altar. Throughout this ambulatory, were massive stained-glass windows, again to let in more light, surrounding smaller chapels that housed saintly relics (Smarthistory, 2020). These chapels were possible through the use of rib vaulting with pointed arches. They opened up the space and allowed for more windows, and thus more sunlight. The features Suger contracted were instrumental for future architects of the Gothic Era and we see them repeated as the period progresses (Ashworth, 2022). The details and functions of these decorative features will be addressed in another section below, but it is important to note that the main purpose for these buildings was to create a terrestrial environment that felt like heaven, mainly through the use of vertically open spaces and light. Dr. Steven Zucker points out that Suger's beliefs were in contrast to other theologians of his time, who believed that decorative features would distract one from their connection to God. Suger's theory was that these decorative features would serve as a conduit rather than a distraction and thus transported you to the heavens (Smarthistory, 2020).

Influences on Gothic Art and Architecture

Gothic art was heavily influenced by other styles of architecture that were popular prior to the Gothic era. The earliest style of architecture that inspired the Gothic era was from the Byzantine empire. Beginning in the fourth century and lasting for one thousand years, the Byzantine empire would influence the Gothic era in both art and architecture. We see Christian-themed art, flying buttresses, vaulting, naturalistic art styles, and mosaics found in Byzantine churches echoed in later Gothic designs. Mosaics were designed to reflect light creating a sense of earthly divinity, which was the same conceptual approach to the churches in the Gothic era. Some examples of Byzantine art that remained influential through the Gothic era were illuminated manuscripts, icon painting (the painting of religious figures), small-scale sculptures, and the shimmering mosaics (The Art Story, n.d.).

Another example of an architectural style that influenced Gothic architecture was Middle Eastern architecture. The pointed arch, found in Islamic structures such as the Al-Aqsa Mosque, in the Al-Ukhaidir palace (The Art Story, n.d.), and in the Dome of the Rock (Darke, 2023) appeared in the 7th century, and continued in popularity in Islamic religious buildings until it was appropriated by European architects in the Gothic Era. Darke (2023) notes that this was not the only architectural feature that was stolen. Rib vaulting, which is created with intersecting pointed arches as well as a trefoil, were also distinctly Islamic.

The third major influence on Gothic era art and architecture was the Romanesque style, popular in the mid-11th century. The Romanesque style featured churches with massive interiors intended to accommodate more devotees such as monks, priests, and those on pilgrimages. It was increasingly common for more individuals to practice a monastic lifestyle, and existing places of worship were no longer sufficient with their smaller interiors and wooden construction materials. Romanesque churches housed not only a lot more people, but relics of saints and had to be made from fire-resistant materials to protect these relics and parishioners. Walls were made from masonry materials and were much thicker than the wooden materials they replaced (Britannica, 2023). The architecture of the Romanesque period featured doors and windows with rounded, semicircular arches, barrel and groin vaulting, pillars, and piers. Gothic churches followed a similar pattern as the Romanesque churches with their entrances that faced west. Other architectural features were repeated at the entrance such as the tower structures, portals, and sculptures (The Art Story, n.d.). Circular windows of the Romanesque period were replaced by rose windows with the earliest example of this in the Basilica of Saint Denis (Sack, 2022).

Features of Gothic Architecture

The churches of the Gothic Era were built to towering new heights than ever before. In order to support the weight of these new heights, flying buttresses were used externally, acting as a "load-bearing skeleton," (Smith, n.p.) Chapius (2002), traces the appearance of flying buttresses in Gothic architecture to the 1170s. She notes that their framework, made of a pier and an arch that extends, or "flies" to the main building supported the weight just below the roof and acted as a support system for any outward thrust of the interior vaults. The flying buttresses of the Notre Dame in Paris were the first used in this era (Clark & Mark, 1984).

New vaulting innovations facilitated an openness, which as a matter of course, allowed more natural light into the space. The previous period's Romanesque barrel vaulting, with its rounded arches, required thick walls to support the outward thrust that resulted from this style. Consequently, the windows that accompanied this style were much smaller because they could not be placed on such thick walls. Pointed arches were a ground-breaking solution. The Art Story (n.d.) describes various styles of a pointed arch, all of which have their roots in Middle Eastern architecture of Islamic religious buildings. A lancet arch, named so because of its resemblance to a lance blade, was a sharply pointed top and was long and narrow. In contrast, an equilateral arch was much wider. The third type of arch, a flamboyant arch, functioned to facilitate a decorative aspect.

Contrary to a semi-circular barrel-shaped arch, or even a groin arch which was made of four intersecting barrel arches, pointed arches did not require thick walls (Chapuis, 2002). The pointed arch directed any weight needed to support it downward rather than outward, so the sides were free from imposing thick walls. Four pointed arches created a rib vault when they were intersected, another architectural feature that allowed for more openness with loftier height. The vaulting was supported by a thin vertical column, which drew the eyes upwards towards the heavens. This highlights the idea that churches of this era replicated a heavenly environment (Smarthistory, 2020).

New structural designs and the use of stone masonry rather than timber allowed for bigger windows, and in Gothic architecture, these windows were made from stained glass. The artistry of stained glass is an elaborate process. It took many steps and many months to complete the beautiful, colorful, and intricate windows that adorned the Gothic cathedrals of this era. A board with a full-sized drawing of the window's design was used as a pattern for the numerous glass pieces that were needed to complete the window. They then made the glass in the colors they needed for the design. Sand and potash were melted together at extremely hot temperatures and coloured with powders such as copper oxide, cobalt, and gold. These metallic powders produced green, blue, cobalt, red, and violet. The glass would then be formed into sheets and the smaller pieces were broken from these sheets to follow the pattern on the board by approximating the sizes and shapes of the details in the designs. For a more precise shape, the artist would use a tool to smooth out the edges in a method referred to as grozing. With the basic shapes in place, the artist could then paint in the details with a special compound made from fine ground glass, bits of iron, and wine or urine. To complete the window's construction, the glass pieces were framed with strips of lead and soldered together. Finished panels were then put together to form the windows, whether they were lancet windows to fit a pointed arch, or a rose window that would typically adorn a cathedral's west entrance (Reynold, 2013).

These windows were appreciated not just for their beauty and ability to shine divine light, but for their educational value. Since only a small percentage of the population were able to read, or who even had authority to read the bible, the stories depicted in the stained-glass window designs acted as a teaching method, allowing patrons to learn these bible stories. Some of the well-known French churches such as the Notre-Dame Cathedral, Sainte-Chapelle, and the Chartres Cathedral, depict a specific biblical tale telling the lineage of kings from Jesse all the way to Christ in a motif referred to as the "Tree of Jesse" (Reynold, 3). Reynolds (2013), points out another common theme in Gothic stained-glass windows. Multiples, specifically the number seven, are frequently seen to represent heavenly gifts or prophets. In the rose window of the Notre-Dame Cathedral, multiples of four, twelve, and twenty-four are used to represent prophets, kings, and judges.

Cathedrals and churches of the Gothic Era featured a distinct window, usually at its western façade above the entrance called a rose window.

Some cathedrals have multiple rose windows at the southern or northern façades. These windows were circle-shaped and made from stone tracery, another innovative technique. Using this method of stone masonry meant that the builders could use more stained-glass panels than the previous era's smaller circular windows (Smith, 2020). A rose window's central image would be that of Christ or of Madonna and child. Reynolds (2013) notes that who was at the center of the rose window would depend on which façade of the cathedral we were looking at. Eastern windows would feature Mary and child to represent birth, or the beginning, much like the way the sun rises in the east. The opposite façade would depict Christ and the final judgment, or the end as the sun sets in the west.

The radiating panels of a rose window would feature the signs of the zodiac or kings and prophets of the Old Testament, and scenes from the bible, as seen in the remarkable rose windows of the Notre-Dame Cathedral in Paris. Notre-Dame's south rose window was built by architects Jean de Chelles and Pierre de Montreuil in the mid 13th century and features the theme of the Last Judgment. The south rose window is 42 feet in diameter (Friends of Notre-Dame de Paris, 2022).

Gargoyles are another distinct feature of Gothic architecture. They were designed as water spouts and they were not only decorative, but functional. Their spouts protruded several feet from the building and they diverted and drained water to prevent damage. They were typically carved animals such as a bird and sometimes they were grotesque beasts. The spout where the water drained was the creature's mouth (Britannica, 2021). Conversely, the faces and characters that served no function other than to be purely decorative were called grotesques or chimeras as seen at the Notre Dame Cathedral (Friends of Notre-Dame de Paris, 2022).

Phases and Styles of Gothic Architecture

Gothic architecture went through three distinctive phases and from these phases, emerged two unique styles. The phases were the Early Gothic, High Gothic, and Late Gothic. The styles were the Rayonnant and the Flamboyant (The Art Story, n.d.).

The Early Gothic spanned approximately fifty years from c. 1120 CE to the turn of the century. With its roots embedded in Abbot Suger's Saint Denis Cathedral, the buildings that followed it were also for religious purposes, and also located in France. These magnificent structures were possible because the economic success of the urban populations meant there was a lot of money that could be spent to build them. The new style of vaulting to allow for more windows was firmly established in this period. The layout of the churches included a clerestory, which was an upper story made of windows. The Early Gothic style spread to other countries, and each region had their own interpretation that set them apart from others. For example, some Gothic churches of England forewent pointed arches and continued with rounded ones that necessitated a thick wall. Others paled in comparison to the French churches in terms of height (Britannica, 2022).

The High Gothic phase is the period from which the **Rayonnant** style first developed in France. This style is what was referred to as Decorated Gothic in England (Britannica, 2023), and then it evolved into the Flamboyant style. This period began at the turn of the 13th century in 1200 CE and lasted for eighty years. It is in this period that the flying buttresses were facilitating the towering heights of the cathedrals. Additionally, spires and pinnacles were added to increase height. Stained glass art became more impressive with its use of tracery to give a more decorative effect. Small-scale sculptures emerged in this period, and the figures depicted in all forms of art began to take on a more naturalistic appearance than earlier pieces that typically featured more frontal views, all typical features of the Rayonnant style (The Art Story, n.d., Britannica, 2022). The Rayonnant style is credited to architect Hugues Libergier, who was known for breaking up a panel of glass with a lot of decorative tracery. The result was a pattern of sunlight that came through the windows, emanating rays, and the style was aptly named for this effect (The Art Story, n.d.).

By the time the High Gothic period ended in 1280, the Rayonnant style developed even more elaborate features than before with more windows and tracery. The tracery was used to decorate more than just windows as it spilled into other stone-built parts of churches. We also saw exaggerated pointed arches that resembled flames. Named for this feature, the Flamboyant style became the dominant aesthetic and thus began the Late Gothic period which lasted until approximately 1500 CE. The Flamboyant style was not reserved for religious buildings, or even businesses or community buildings. Private residences were decorated using Flamboyant features. As previously mentioned, different countries had their own unique version of the different styles. England's application of Flamboyant was called Perpendicular style and used a new form of vaulting that resulted from the overuse of tracery. Resembling a fan, it was called fan vaulting (Britannica, 2022).

Other Works of Art

The influence of the Byzantine Empire on art can be seen not just with smaller, more portable sculptures, but with paintings and illuminated manuscripts. Gold was used in paintings, which gave a glistening effect, much like the mosaics from the Byzantine era (Britannica, 2022). Illuminated manuscripts, which in simple terms were religious books with illustrations were also found in both periods. Some of these religious texts were Books of Hours, small prayer books filled with little paintings to accompany the text and helped tell the stories within (The Art Story, n.d.).

Conclusion

Spanning approximately four hundred years, the Gothic Era made its mark in history with its grand cathedrals. Innovative architectural techniques combined with influences of the past took the interiors to soaring new heights and made room for even more decorative features than ever before. So magnificent and detailed was this architecture, that it was considered art on its own. Gothic art and architecture would have such an impact on history, that it inspired a new genre of literature when the style was revived centuries later. The pointed arches, beautiful stained-glass windows, gargoyles, and the like are still very much appreciated by architecture enthusiasts today.

References

Ashworth, W. B. (2022, March 11). Abbot suger. The Linda Hall Library. Retrieved from https://www.lindahall.org/about/news/scientist-of-the-day/abbot-suger

Britannica, T. Editors of Encyclopaedia (2022, September 3). Gothic art. Encyclopedia Britannica. https://www.britannica.com/art/Gothic-art

Britannica, T. Editors of Encyclopaedia (2021, September 6). gargoyle. Encyclopedia Britannica. https://www.britannica.com/technology/gargoyle

Britannica, T. Editors of Encyclopaedia (2022, July 26). Giorgio Vasari. Encyclopedia Britannica. https://www.britannica.com/biography/Giorgio-Vasari

Britannica, T. Editors of Encyclopaedia (2023, February 10). Romanesque architecture. Encyclopedia Britannica. https://www.britannica.com/art/Romanesque-architecture

Byzantine art and architecture overview. The Art Story. (n.d.). Retrieved February 26, 2023, from https://www.theartstory.org/movement/byzantine-art/

Chapuis, J. 2002. Gothic Art. In Heilbrunn Timeline of Art History. New York: The Metropolitan Museum of Art, 2000–. http://www.metmuseum.org/toah/hd/mgot/hd_mgot.htm

Clark, W. W., & Mark, R. (1984). The First Flying Buttresses: A New Reconstruction of the Nave of Notre-Dame de Paris. The Art Bulletin, 66(1), 47–65. https://doi.org/10.2307/3050392

Darke, D. (2023, February 24). Stealing from the Saracens: How islamic architecture shaped europe. Middle East Institute. Retrieved from https://www.mei.edu/publications/stealing-saracens-how-islamic-architecture-shaped-europe

Gothic art and architecture overview. The Art Story. (n.d.). Retrieved from https://www.theartstory.org/movement/gothic-art-and-architecture/

Mark, J. J. (2014, October 12). The Goths. World History Encyclopedia. Retrieved from https://www.worldhistory.org/Goths/

Reynolds, Elizabeth (Aislin) (2013) "The Development of Stained Glass in Gothic Cathedrals," JCCC Honors Journal: Vol. 4: Iss. 1, Article 3. Retrieved from http://scholarspace.jccc.edu/honors_journal/vol4/iss1/3

Rockwell, A. F. (2023, January 9). Suger. Encyclopedia Britannica. https://www.britannica.com/biography/Suger

Rose Windows. Friends of Notre-Dame de Paris. (2022, May 6). Retrieved February 19, 2023, from https://www.friendsofnotredamedeparis.org/cathedral/artifacts/rose-windows/

Sack, H. (2022, January 13). Abbot Suger and the birth of the Gothic style. SciHi Blog. Retrieved from http://scihi.org/abbot-suger-gothic-style/

Smarthistory (2020, December 08). Birth of the Gothic: Abbot Suger and the ambulatory at St. Denis. World History Encyclopedia. Retrieved from https://www.worldhistory.org/video/2205/birth-of-the-gothic-abbot-suger-and-the-ambulatory/

Smith, H. (2020, December 08). Gothic Cathedrals: Architecture & Divine Light. World History Encyclopedia. Retrieved from https://www.worldhistory.org/article/1649/gothic-cathedrals-architecture--divine-light/

The Arts and Architecture of Africa

By Naharah Wilmot

Introduction

The art of Africa has a long, rich, history that is quite complex and spans many centuries. It is a topic that appears inexhaustible and requires much time and many pages to adequately depict its vastness, diversity, and beauty. Thus, what this paper intends to do, is to provide a comprehensive overview of the subject while still highlighting the most relevant and enduring aspects of the history of art in Africa. Africa is home to various artistic expressions reflecting the continent's diverse peoples, cultures, and traditions. However, this paper will focus on and examine the major artistic forms that have emerged and evolved over time. To begin we will examine rock art and its contributions to the development of African art. According to the New World Encyclopedia, "the origins of African art lie long before recorded history" (New World Encyclopedia, 2021). In fact, "recently discovered examples of patterned stone, ochre, and ostrich eggshell as well as evidence of personal ornamentation emerging from Middle Stone Age Africa (100,000-60,000 years ago), have demonstrated that "art" is not only a much older phenomenon than previously thought but that it has its roots in the African continent (The British Museum, 2023). Thus, we will begin our exploration with one of the oldest and most significant insights into the history of art in Africa.

Rock Art

"African rock art in the Sahara in present-day Niger preserves 6000-year-old carvings [and] the earliest known sculptures are from the Nok culture of Nigeria, made around 500 B.C.E." (New World Encyclopedia, "History heading," 2021). "A summary of rock art databases in Southern African countries indicate that there are at least 14,000 sites on record, but that many more exist than have been formally recorded" (Deacon, 1997, as cited in Deacon, 2002) and perhaps even discovered. Interestingly, "the oldest dated rock art in Africa was discovered in the Apollo 11 Cave in the Huns Mountains in southwestern Namibia. Seven grey-brown quartzite slabs, each smaller than an adult hand, were found with images drawn in charcoal and ochre during excavations in the cave in 1969 by German archaeologist W.E. Wendt. The discovery occurred at the time of the Apollo 11 mission to the moon, and the shelter was given the same name to celebrate the momentous event" (Bradshaw Foundation, 2023). Rock art, itself, is quite diverse and can be referred to as rock paintings, drawings, engravings, and petroglyphs. The different names reflect the varying styles, materials, and techniques employed by the artists in creating this art in various parts of the continent. As an example, "rock paintings make use of natural pigments, such as ochre or charcoal, applied to the surface of the rocks using brushes or other tools" (Coulson, 2001). While "rock engravings are made by chipping away at the surface of the rock to create a design, often using stone tools or metal implements" (Chippindale & Tacon, 1998). And lastly, "petroglyphs are a type of rock art that involves the use of carved or incised designs, rather than painted or engraved ones" (Bednarik, 2001).

The Significance of Rock Art

Rock art is significant for several reasons but here we will focus on the historical, cultural, and spiritual aspects. Rock art is first, a pointer to African pre-historic times. They do this by, "providing evidence of environmental change or recording significant events, such as the introduction of horses and chariots to parts of the Sahara. Rock art depicts animals, such as elephants, hippos, and giraffes that once occurred in the interior of the Sahara but became extinct as the rich Savanna ecosystem turned to [a] desert". (African World Heritage, 2018). It also gives evidence of how people at that time lived, acquired food, and began producing their food.

For example, there was plenty of competition between humans and animals for these resources. Mazel writes, "Baboons and San (Bushmen) competed for a variety of food resources; this is shown in paintings of the humans fighting with and chasing baboons" (2018). Additionally, "the first herders were Stone Age people… until about 2000 years ago all human groups that had ever lived in southern Africa survived entirely by hunting and collecting wild animals and vegetable foods. At about this time, fat-tailed sheep first appeared in southern Africa from further north. This marks the first introduction of an exotic domesticated species – hence the beginning of food production (Mazel, 2018). Another important discovery made was that… "people were making harpoons. This means that they were planning their food-collecting strategies in much more sophisticated ways than had ever been done by other animals or other hominids. They were also making awls and therefore were probably wearing skins for clothing" (Coulson, 2001).

Rock Art and Human and Animal Figure

The rock art found did not just feature drawings of animals, but it also had, "depictions of elegant human figures, richly hued animals, and figures combining human and animal features called "therianthropes" [which have been] associated with shamanism" (The Metropolitan Museum of Art, 2000). These "*therianthropes*… usually have some antelope (especially eland) features. One interpretation of these figures is that the hunters disguised [themselves] as animals to help them in the chase…The San (Bushmen) believe that the eland possesses a powerful mystical force [that] the medicine man draws upon to enable him to enter a trance" (Mazel, 2020). This was very symbolic, in a religious and traditional sense because, "during [these] trance[s] they perform[ed] various mystical tasks such as healing, the purging of evil and rainmaking" (Mazel, 2020). Also, in the way of tradition, "the eland as a symbol is also invoked at important ceremonies [such as] a girl's puberty when the eland bull dance is performed [and] after a boy's first hunt and at marriage (Mazel, 2020). Researchers found that "The Dabous giraffes of Niger [were also an example of this and write] we see creatures that are part-human, part animal; giraffes with lines emanating from their mouths that meander across the rock-face until they finally join to a floating human form and many other mysterious beings (Coulson, 2001). This was thought to have spiritual and ritualistic connotations. Below is an excerpt taken from the Bradshaw Foundation that outlines the spiritual connection that rock art had with the people of that time. It says:

> Far to the south, beyond the great Zambezi River, is the land of the oldest known of all the first peoples: the San or Bushmen. This is the place where, it seems, art began. The more recent San rock paintings and engravings of southern Africa, dating to the past 10,000 years, are amongst the most beautiful and fine of all the world arts in terms of their technique. They are amongst the most complex and sophisticated in terms of symbolism. Far from a general view of life, the art focuses on a particular part of the San experience: the spirit world journeys and experiences of San religious specialists, people we know today as shamans. Thus, we see many features from the all-important trance dance, the venue in which the shamans gained access to the spirit world. We see dancers with antelope hooves, showing that they have taken on antelope power, just as San shamans describe

> in the Kalahari today. Then, we see shamans climbing up the 'threads of light' that connect to the sky-world (Coulson 2001).

As mentioned earlier, there is really no way to define or discuss the art of Africa, without going back to where it all began and first appreciating its origins. To conclude, rock art has great cultural, traditional, and spiritual significance. It is not only a window into the various artistic expressions present back then, but it provides insight into spiritual and cultural practices, historical roots, and the general ways of living prevalent at that time. Now that we know all about rock art, let's take a look at other art forms from Ancient Africa.

Other Forms of Art

Before we dive into some other types of art, one important thing to be noted about African art is, its three-dimensionality. And sources seem to agree that this was unique to African artists. The New World Encyclopedia reports that "even many African paintings or cloth work were meant to be experienced three-dimensionally" (2020). For example, "house paintings are often seen as a continuous design wrapped around a house, forcing the viewer to walk around the work to experience it fully; while decorated cloths are worn as decorative or ceremonial garments, transforming the wearer into a living sculpture" (New World Encyclopedia, 2021). Thus, we will first take a look at sculptures.

Sculptures:

"Sculpture was one of the most important types of art in Ancient Africa. Sculptures were mostly made of people and sometimes animals. African artists often used wood for their sculptures, but they also used bronze, terracotta, and ivory" (Ducksters, 2023). And according to The Britannica Encyclopedia, "stone sculpture occurs in several separate centres, employing both hard and soft rock, but there is usually not much evidence of development through time in a single place (2023). Generally, the material of choice for these sculptures was wood, "but an adz, with its cutting edge at right angles to the shaft, [was] used for the substantive work of carving…[however] more intricate work [was] done with knives (Britannica, 2023).

Masks:

Masks are yet another imperative area of discussion when it comes to African art forms and, "they were often used together with dance to create a type of performance art (Ducksters, 2023). Again, these marks we typically made from wood and would "represent either human[s] or animal[s], [they were also known to be], "one of the most commonly found forms of art in western Africa…used for celebrations, initiations, crop harvesting, and war preparation (New World Encyclopedia, 2021).

Jewelry:

Jewelry was also a significant way in which African art was expressed. Some of the materials used to create this jewelry include "gold, gems, and shells… [and this was] an important part of showing one's status and wealth" (Ducksters, 2023). Additionally, "the jewelry of Africa is not just ornamental" (Camera, 2019). African Jewelry, just like the aforementioned art forms, plays a role in their culture and spirituality as well. "For each group, rituals and religion play a major part in the adornment of jewelry. Each piece is represented and worn for a particular reason, ranging from aesthetics to identifying marks of a society or group. The climate also has a lot to do with the materials used to make the jewelry" (Camera, 2019).

Pottery:

Lastly, we will discuss pottery. In general, "ceramics were used for everyday items like bowls and cooking pots. However, some ceramics were works of art that were shaped and painted with fine details

(Ducksters, 2023). It is believed that "people in East Africa started to make clay pots about 6000BC…[and] by 400 BC, pottery making had spread as far west as West Africa" (Carr, 2017).

The Architecture of Africa

Introduction

African architecture is just as expansive and diverse as its art and in fact, it is considered a part of Africa's visual arts. According to the Britannica Encyclopedia, "discussions of architecture in sub-Saharan Africa focus chiefly on housing in villages, rural mosques, and the melange of colonial and modern influences that characterize urban areas" (Britannica, 2022). However, in terms of history, certain challenges exist in determining accurate historical information. This is so because of "…intellectual historiography that bifurcates the continent into two parts comprising an "uncivilized" black Africa occupying sub-Saharan regions and an Arab North Africa fairly 'civilized" because of its proximity to the Western civilizations of the Mediterranean region and southern Europe" (Architecture- Africa- the roots of indigenous African Architecture n.d.). Thus, once again, this paper will provide a brief overview that attempts to highlight the most significant aspects of architecture in Africa.

History

According to African Architecture, "recent discoveries of stone structures in southern Africa are argued to be the earliest human-made buildings on the planet, dating back 75,000 years" (2015). Additionally, there is evidence suggesting that "the Soninke people of pre-historical Ghana had… architects who carved stone masonry settlements and worked with copper as early as 2500 BCE (African Architecture, 2015). Still, several sources agree that "the most well-known architectural wonders of Africa are those in ancient Egypt, including the monumental obelisks, the pyramids at Giza, and the Great Sphinx from the period between 2000 BCE and 100 CE (African Architecture, 2015).

African Architecture

The materials used in architectural constructions in Africa were quite varied. And in terms of characteristics, "it reflects the interaction of environmental factors such as natural resources, climate, and vegetation, with the economies and population densities of the continent's various regions [thus] ...the overwhelming majority of Africa's thousands of peoples in rural areas build in grasses, wood, and clay" (African Architecture, Geographic influences n.d.).

The excerpt below taken from African Architecture gives further insight into some of the different materials used in construction:

> In Ghana, West Africa, and Ethiopia, tombs and monuments dating back as early as 1000 BCE were erected from carved stone. Often, entire temples would be carved from a single block of rock, such as in Tigray. It was common for most buildings to be created from local materials such as timber, mudbrick, or limestone. One of the trademarks of Aksumite architecture was constructed from layers of mud and wood in a unique design that came to be known as "monkey head" support beams (2015).

Ancient African Architecture: History and examples, also gives some important insight:

> The earliest African dwellings were carved out of solid rock. Later dwellings were constructed of animal skins, and still later, wattle and daub, a framework of woven sticks covered with a layer of mud to seal the dwelling from the elements. Later, mudbricks, or mud compressed into bricks, sometimes combined with straw, became the building material of choice. Dating when mudbrick was first used is difficult; however, it is still used in some regions today. Mudbrick allowed builders to construct larger, more spacious buildings. However, these

constructions did not withstand the elements well, so few ancient mudbrick buildings remain intact. An example of ancient mudbrick construction is the city of Kerma. Kerma was settled around 2400 BCE and is one of the largest archeological sites in Nubia, which is present-day Sudan (Ancient African Architecture: History and Examples, 2018).

However, as the influences from other places started to spread, "Africans began using marble and Roman arches. During the first millennia CE, African art and architecture were heavily influenced by Christian and Muslim Traders, conquerors, and settlers" (African Architecture, 2015). This and other influences continued and grew, so much so that, "throughout northern Africa and as far west as Morocco, Islamic architectural design influenced traditional African buildings. [And] by 1000 CE, Mosaic-tiled mosques begin to appear in African cities alongside stone Christian churches" (African Architecture, 2015).

Egyptian Architecture:

We will now explore the connection between African architecture and Egypt. According to African Architecture, "the best-known African architecture comes from Egypt [which] at the time of the pyramids was the richest part of Africa because of its location along the Nile River and its close proximity to the Mediterranean Sea" (Ancient African Architecture, 2022). [And a common thought when it comes to Egyptian architecture is that the] "great pyramids and temples… were built by people whose skin colour was lighter than the complexion of people who reside in sub-Saharan Africa" (2022). However, there is archaeological evidence that strongly argues that "early Egyptian dynasties and their monumental architecture were built by ancient African kings" (2022). Thus, we will further discuss the influence of Egyptian architecture with an understanding that, "indigenous

African architecture includes pyramids, temples, clay structures, tent structures, huts made of grass and reeds, and a combination of multiple building materials, and the tectonics of each structure depended on its geographical location and the time in which it was conceived and produced" (African Architecture, 2015). This is important because it, "emphasises [the fact] that monumental architecture such as the pyramids did not just develop in ancient Egypt overnight… [But more accurately] it evolved slowly following the desiccation of the Sahara Desert, whereupon certain building traditions from the Sahara were transferred to the newly founded kingdom of Egypt by Menes the pharaoh whom archeologists identify as Narmer (African Architecture, 2015).

Construction of Egyptian Architecture:

Below is a description of how early Egyptian Architecture was constructed, this excerpt is taken from Ancient African Architecture: History & Examples:

> Early Egyptian architecture was primarily from stone because this material was readily available. The oldest building, a stepped stone pyramid, dates to around 2650 BCE and is part of the necropolis, or cemetery, on the Nile shore opposite the ancient city of Memphis, the first Egyptian capital. The structure may have started out as a mastaba, a rectangular, flat-topped building with sloping sides. Mastabas were tombs or burial chambers, usually built for Egyptian pharaohs or rulers. Archaeologists believe the step pyramid was expanded upward to create the six-layered pyramid. Because these early tombs were built solid with tunnels to get to the various chambers, archaeologists estimate that builders used 11.6 million cubic feet of limestone to construct the step pyramid. As Egyptian builders became more skilled, the tombs of the pharaohs became more complex, made with blocks of stone that fit together almost

seamlessly and with smoothly sloped sides. By 2500 BCE, Egyptian tombs became more polished, such as the pyramids of Giza, but they were still a solid construction laced with tunnels. (Ancient African Architecture: History & Examples, 2018)

Conclusion:

African architecture has a rich and diverse history that is entwined with the influences of various cultures. The styles and techniques employed to construct these buildings have evolved over the years and remain an area of study and interest even today. The ancient pyramids of Egypt were discussed, in addition to the mudbrick structures. We looked at the very first rock and stone constructions and the various other materials and tools engaged to build these structures. We spent time looking at early Egyptian architecture, its complexity and intricacy, and its role in defining African architecture. And finally, it was understood that African architecture had strong cultural, spiritual, and geographical significance in ancient times, impacts that are still being felt today and likely for many years to come.

References

Architecture (2023). Africa, The Roots of Indigenous African Architecture. (n.d.). Architecture - Africa - the Roots of Indigenous African Architecture - Ancient, History, Egyptian, and Saharan - JRank Articles. https://science.jrank.org/pages/8352/Architecture-Africa-Roots-Indigenous-African-Architecture.html

Ancient African Architecture: History & Examples. (2018). Study.com. https://study.com/academy/lesson/ancient-african-architecture-history-examples.html#:~:text=The%20earliest%20African%20dwellings%20were,the%20dwelling%20from%20the%20elements.

African Architecture. (2015, November 23). Highbrow. https://gohighbrow.com/african-architecture/#:~:text=Africans%20began%20using%20marble%20and,design%20influenced%20traditional%20African%20buildings.

African Art. (2021, April 30). New World Encyclopedia, Retrieved, February 18, 2023, from https://www.newworldencyclopedia.org/p/index.php?title=African_Art&oldid=1052072.

African World Heritage Sites. (2018). Rock Art & Pre-History. February 18, 2023.https://www.africanworldheritagesites.org/cultural-places/rock-art-pre-history.html#:~:text=In%20many%20areas%20they%20trace,to%20parts%20of%20the%20Sahara

African Rock Art. (2000). The Metropolitan Museum of Art. Retrieved, February 18, 2023. https://www.metmuseum.org/toah/hd/rock/hd_rock.htm

Africa Rock Art Archive. (2023). Where is the oldest rock art? Bradshaw Foundation. February 18, 2023. https://www.bradshawfoundation.com/africa/oldest_art/index.php

Bednarik, R. G. (2001). The distinction between petroglyphs and rock engravings. Rock Art Research, 18 (1), 79-81. https://www.researchgate.net/publication/349624331_Ethnographic_interpretation_of_rock_art_through_rock_inscriptions

Britannica, T. Editors of Encyclopaedia (2022, October 7). Renaissance architecture. Encyclopedia Britannica. https://www.britannica.com/art/Renaissance-architecture

Britannica. (2023). Sculpture and associated arts. Encyclopedia Britannia, Inc. Retrieved on February 18, 2023. https://www.britannica.com/art/African-art/Sculpture-and-associated-arts

Carr, Karen. (2017). Early African Pottery. Quatr.us Study Guides. https://quatr.us/african-history/early-african-pottery.htm#:~:text=People%20in%20East%20Africa%20started,and%20Yoruba%20potters%20made%20pottery.

Camera, Lucille. (2019). The History and Aesthetics of African Jewelry. Yale New-Haven Teachers Institute. Curriculum Units by Fellows of the Yale-New Haven Teachers Institute 1993 Volume IV: The Minority Artist in America. https://teachersinstitute.yale.edu/curriculum/units/files/93.04.02.pdf

Chippindale, C., & Tacon, S.C. (1998). The archaeology of rock art. Cambridge University Press. https://www.researchgate.net/publication/310752272_An_archaeology_of_rock_art_through_informed_methods_and_formal_methods

Coulson, David. (2001). The Rock Art of Africa. The common heritage of humanity. https://www.bradshawfoundation.com/africa/african_rock_art/index.php

Deacon, Janette (2002). “Southern African Rock Art Sites”. In collaboration with members of the Southern African Rock Art Project (SARAP). International Council on Monuments and Sites. https://www.icomos.org/en/116-english-categories/resources/publications/227-southern-african-rock-art-sites

Deacon, Janette (2002). "Southern African Rock Art Sites". In collaboration with members of the Southern African Rock Art Project (SARAP). International Council on Monuments and Sites. https://www.icomos.org/en/116-english-categories/resources/publications/227-southern-african-rock-art-sites

Ducksters. (2023). Ancient Africa for kids: Art. Ducksters. Retrieved from https://www.ducksters.com/history/africa/ancient_african_art.php
Origins of Rock Art in Africa. (2023). The Trustees of the British Museum, Retrieved, February 18, 2023. https://africanrockart.britishmuseum.org/introduction/origins/

Mazel, Aron. (2020). Animals in Rock Art. Bradshaw Foundation. Retrieved, February 18th, 2023. https://www.bradshawfoundation.com/rockartnetwork/maggs_mazel.php

Modernist art and Architecture of the 20th Century

By Sophia Kazakoff

The modernist art and architecture movement of the 20th century was viewed as a both an art and philosophical movement. Modernism is what defined a break from traditional forms and a departure towards a new era of aesthetic expression. This analysis will explore modernist art and its significant movements such as cubism, futurism, and abstract expressionism. Furthermore we will analyze the contributions of key artists such as Pablo Picasso, Georges Braque. Additionally, we will also explore modernist architecture and the various movements and aspects that went into the modernist architecture movement. Our analysis will include an overview of how the movement catalyzed, including an in depth overview of the Bauhaus School and its impact. Furthermore, influential icons such as Walter Gropius will also be discussed. Additionally, this analysis will also include a discussion on current architecture that features modernist styles, designs, and themes. There will be a thorough analysis on how the current trend of designing rural retreats features minimalist approaches that reject ornamentation and excessiveness, and incorporate the background of nature as a contrast to the property itself. Furthermore, there will also be a case study of sorts on how the influence of modernist architecture has spread far beyond the scope of western society. There will be a breakdown of the conceptual grounding, key themes in architecture that set a definitive era in modernist architecture in West Africa, and how the rise and demise of modernist architecture could be attributed to socio-political, economic and various other reasons.

To give some background information on what modernism is, an excellent resource is the overview provided by "Art in Context". Modernism is known as a global movement that existed in society and culture, which started in the early 20th century in response to widespread urbanization that appeared after the industrial revolution. Modern Art, or Modernism reflected societies desires from artists to produce novel forms of social structures, art, and philosophy that paralleled the innovation and development of the newly developing world (artincontext, 2022). Furthermore, to channel these novel themes in art and architecture, artists and architects adapted techniques and principles that dismissed history and traditional concepts associated with realism. These new techniques and principles came in many forms, examples include Post-Impressionism, Fauvism, Cubism, Dadaism, Expressionism, and Futurism to name a few (artincontext, 2022). Additionally, one parallel concept that was present through all of the modernist themes was the principle of breaking away from the customs of traditional, representational art. A main catalyst and influence for modernism was the impressionism movement, which involved the use of non-naturalistic colors when depicting subjects (artincontext, 2022). To add more context to impressionism, it was significantly unpopular with high society at the time, the main reason being that it embraced elements that did not fit into the traditional way of making art (artincontext, 2022). Additionally, the embrace of abstract tendencies getting incorporated into art lead to a further deviation from the norm leading to a wide array of style yet to be explored (artincontext, 2022).

"Paintings are flat, sculptures are 3-dimensional. Why cannot paintings be made to see things from different directions?"

- Pablo Picasso

There could not be a discussion on modernism or modern art without the mention of the Cubist movement within modernism, and especially considering the impact of Pablo Picasso and Georges Braque (C. M, 2023). Cubism is known as the modernist art style founded by both Picasso and Barque – created out of dissatisfaction and drawn out of inspiration from Paul Cezanne, an artist who is known for taking simple forms and developing better ways of presenting them (C. M, 2023). However, unlike Cezanne, Picasso didn't use the simplified shapes and sharp lines to add depth but instead he broke subject down into other geometric forms. Additionally, Picasso reconstructed the subjects with different segments that encompassed all angles of the subjects for the viewers perspective. Moreover, as a style in itself, Cubism was not meant to be or appear life-like or realistic in any way, it is however, a way for conventional still life, landscape, and portrait painting to be revolutionized through abstraction (C. M, 2023). In terms of the different styles in the artform of Cubism, there are two major phases: Analytical Cubism and Synthetic Cubism (C. M, 2023). The main difference between the two is that Analytical Cubism focuses on the form of the subjects which then follows a reconstruction of the subject but with geometric shapes. Additionally, color was either dull or even entirely absent (C. M, 2023). Conversely, Synthetic Cubism is the later phase of Cubism that revolved around the experimental nature of collage. Synthetic Cubism is focused on a merger of great amount of subject matter including textures, surfaces, and other collage elements (C. M, 2023). To analyze more of the differences between the two movements it is also important to observe how Analytical Cubism uses basic geometric shapes such as cubes, pyramids, spheres, cylinders etc. to represent the natural world while Synthetic Cubism uses textures and collages. All in all, Cubism has been and will remain as one of the most iconic style in Modernism and Modern Art – by influencing and composing a substantial portion of modernism in general, Cubism is a timeless art form that will continue to inspire (C. M, 2023).

Futurism

Futurism was an art movement from Italy throughout the early twentieth century that aimed to capture the dynamism and energy of the modern world (Tate, 2023). Founded by Italian poet Filippo Tommaso Marinetti, the futurist movement was vehement in the denunciation of the past. To add more cultural context, the view people had on Italy's past was felt as oppressive (Tate, 2023). In the manifesto written by Marinetti himself, he asserted that "we will free Italy from her innumerable museums which cover her like countless cemeteries" – A quote reflective of his personal stance on the Italy's past (Tate, 2023). In terms of styles and techniques, futurist paintings used elements of neo-impressionism and cubism to express the various elements of modern life including, but not limited to dynamism, energy, and movement (Tate, 2023). Some notable mentions that were renowned for their unique individual style in futurism were Giacomo Balla, Umberto Boccioni, Gino Severini (Tate, 2023). Furthermore, a style that is similar to futurism that is also regarded as the British equivalent is known as Vorticism, however the founder Wyndham Lewis was a overt critique of futurism (Tate, 2023). A major turning point in futurism was the cultural significance of the first world war. After the war was over, many artists took a stance against avant-garde notions of futurism and subsequent pre-war movements and adopting more traditional and reassuring approaches, also referred to as the "return to order" (Tate, 2023).

Abstract Expressionism

A style emerging out of New York City, abstract expressionists were known as the New York School (Tate, 2023). Inspired by the surrealist idea of art emerge from the unconscious mind, abstract expressionists prioritize the aim creating art though expressive and emotional techniques (Tate, 2023). Abstract expressionism follows two broad groupings, the action painters – who utilize aggressive and expressive brush strokes on their canvases; and the field painters – who cover their canvases with large areas of single colors (Tate, 2023). The two substantially influential leaders in action painting were Jackson Pollock and Willem de Kooning. They were both known to work in spontaneous improvisatory manners by using large brushes and making gestural marks (Tate, 2023). Pollock even said on record that he prefers to place his canvas on the ground and dance around while pouring paint from a can and trailing it with a brush or stick, placing his impulses into art form. In terms of other influential leaders involved in abstract expressionism, Mark Rothko, Barnett Newman, and Clyfford Still take the most influential positions (Tate, 2023). With the main focus being on religion and myth, they explored in simple compositions of large areas of color that were intended to produce a contemplative or meditational response in the viewer. An example of this focus would be an essay written in 1948 where he states: “Instead of making cathedrals out of Christ, man, or life, we are making it out ourselves, out of our own feelings” (Tate, 2023). This was of thinking was demonstrated throughout the 1960s as it became more developed and lead to color field painting, a major part of abstract expressionism – where large areas are covered by a single flat color (Tate, 2023).

Modernism and Modern art in general has also had a profound impact on society (Larson, 2019). Throughout history the definition of art remained very flexible, but with the introduction of modernity and modern art it became even more flexible (Larson, 2019). The usual forms of art throughout culture have been painting, graphics, sculpture, architecture, theater, dance, cinema, music, literature and many more, however through modernism, other types of art have appeared. In the 20th and 21st century there has been an explosive trend in photography, video art, and media art (Larson, 2019). With the rapid technological change happening on a constant basis, art has reached a point where the beauty presented is done so in all forms (Larson, 2019). Furthermore, the domain with art merges with technology, creating artifacts and pieces that were not possible to create in the past, and with the use of the internet, it has never been easier to share, visualize and create these artifacts and pieces (Larson, 2019).

Moreover, it is important to make a distinction between modern art and contemporary art as while they might be perceived as similar or even the same style, there are differences (Johnson, J, 2015). Firstly, it's important to note that modern art has laid the foundation for contemporary art since both have developed into major trends due to technological advancements (Johnson, J, 2019). While modern art is revolving around futurism, cubism, abstract expressionism and pop art, contemporary art is far less well defined (Johnson, J, 2019). Contemporary art is a style regarded as belonging to artists still living today. Additionally, contemporary art has begun incorporating new mediums to match technological and resource advancements of today's day and age with video art, site-specific art, and installation art being a few examples (Johnson, J, 2019).

The Modernist architecture movement on the other hand put emphasis on other style and design priorities. By rejecting ornament and embracing minimalism, Modernism is renowned as the single most important new style or philosophy of architecture and design of the 20th century (Baldwin, E, 2022). As previously mentioned, the elimination of ornament allowed for a novel, more analytical approach to the function of buildings. Architectural modernism followed a trend of emphasis on volume, asymmetrical compositions, and minimal ornamentation (Baldwin, E, 2022). To outline the significance of the modernist architectural movement, we will be looking at a current example of modernism in architecture and that is of rural retreats. A major aspect of the design of these rural retreats is minimalism (Baldwin, E, 2022). The start of minimalism as an art movement could be dated to World War II, and the point in which it became a major design aesthetic could be traced to the 1960s and 1970s, with major cities like London and New York incorporating it all through the 1980s as well. The following examples are minimalist approaches incorporated into rural settings with the focus being on materials and detailing (Baldwin, E, 2022). The "Small but Fine Cabin" by Studio Politaire is a project that showcases a minimalist effect where the home is arranged in a way where each window looks out to a different view. Located in the secluded landscapes of Scandinavia, this home features four slightly offset rooms that are surrounded by a unique natural landscape. Similarly, to the nature emersed "Small but Fine Cabin", the "Square House" by Studio Puisto is also a home that is surrounded by a densely spruce forest, with a lake landscape opening on the east side (Baldwin, E, 2022). The main parallel to draw from both of these projects is how the minimalism applies to the exterior of the project just as much as the interior (Baldwin, E, 2022). The minimalism is centered around the remoteness of the location of these homes, where the density of nature forms the background, similarly to a canvas, and the homes themselves are the artifacts that stand out despite not being large or ornamented, they stand out due to contrast with that background (Baldwin, E, 2022).

A substantial impact on modernist architecture was the Bauhaus school. Founded in 1919 by architect Walter Gropius in the city of Weimar, Bauhaus would "reimagine the material world to reflect the unity of all the arts", as its core objective (Winton, A. G, 2023). With the guidance of Gropius, the Bauhaus school would incorporate a vision for the union of art and design by incorporating a combination of architecture, sculpture, and painting into a combined and broad expression (Winton, A. G, 2023). What made Bauhaus significantly distinct from other institutions was the holistic approach incorporated in the curriculum. At Bauhaus, students were enrolled in specialized workshops including cabinetmaking, metalworking, pottery, typography, weaving, and wall painting (Winton, A. G, 2023). This curriculum was the attempt of Gropius to unify arts through craft, but after facing financial burdens he switched the traditional aim into an updated "art into industry" approach that paved the way for modernist architecture (Winton, A. G, 2023). A display of the direction that Gropius took when it came to modernism was that when Bauhaus moved locations from Weimar to Dessau in 1925, Gropius would design the new building in a way that would be considered as a hallmark in modernist architecture (Winton, A. G, 2023). The new building housing the Bauhaus school included modernist features such as a steel frame construction, an asymmetrical pinwheel plan, and a glass curtain wall. These modernist features were incorporated with the notion of maximum efficiency and spatial logic to house a studio, classrooms, and an administrative space (Winton, A. G, 2023). Lastly, during World War 2, many of the key figures from Bauhaus emigrated to the US where the would go on and make a great impact on the following generations of young architects and designers (Winton, A. G, 2023).

To link the various aspects of modernist architecture to a case study where a culture outside the western scope adopted the same trends in design but incorporated a uniqueness that is rooted in the domestic culture, we will look at the modernist architecture in West Africa, particularly the aspects of modernist architecture from 1948 to 1970. To gain a detailed insight we will be using an article published by Ola Uduku, titled "Modernist architecture and 'the tropical' in West Africa: The tropical architecture movement in West Africa, 1948-1970". In this article Uduku analyzes the conceptual grounding, key architects and select buildings that define the era (Uduku, 2006). Furthermore, many of the important socio-political, economic and aesthetic reasons for the movements rise as well as demise are also explored (Uduku,

2006). An argument is also made that Tropical Architecture produced in British West Africa had similarities and a sort of resonance with the global phenomenon of tropical architecture in the 1950s (Uduku, 2006). Key elements from the article that highlight the significant impact of modernist architecture in a West African context are how the modernist or tropical architecture movement in West Africa is known to be robust and long-lasting, how most of the buildings of the era are over half a century old yet are still in use, and how this trend of design was founded on the principle of designing for and with the climate conditions present (Uduku, 2006). Additionally, the text also highlights how the modernist and tropical design trends have also lead as initiative in sustainable building, with an example being the Arup-sustainably engineered office block in Harare, where the design incorporates a variety of green features and a passive cooling system. Furthermore, in terms of modernist architecture following a different and unique path in West Africa, Uduku made it apparent in his analysis that West Africa has seen a renewed interest in designing buildings that have a localized, regional design response, where building using indigenous or vernacular styles create a unique climatic and environmental design response. Overall, the study of modernist architecture in West Africa allow us to have a holistic, and an in depth view on how modernism can be appropriated to a unique culture (Uduku, 2006).

Overall, in the context of modernism in art, modern art reflected society's desire for artists to produce new forms of social structures, are and philosophy which paralleled the innovation and development of the newly developing world. With the foundation of the movement being grounded in breaking away from traditionalism, modern art incorporated representational themes throughout its movement. Cubism, one of the most iconic styles of modern art, revolutionized landscape, still life, and portrait painting through the use of abstraction. Futurism, founded by Italian poet Filippo Tommaso Marinetti, aimed at capturing the dynamism and energy of the modern world using neo-impressionism and cubist techniques. Modernist art in general was a significant stride in challenging conventional art concepts, later laying the foundation for other forms of contemporary art. Furthermore, modernist architecture is a style and trend that emerged in the 20th century. With a strong emphasis on minimalism, volume, asymmetrical compositions, and functionality, modernist architecture rejected excessiveness and ornamentation. Additionally, the Bauhaus school played a significant role in the development of modernist architecture by promoting a holistic approach by integrating craft, art and design into architecture. Modernist architecture also emerged outside of the Western scope of influence, with buildings getting built in West Africa that followed their own principle of modernism of designing for climate conditions present and following the interest of localized and regional design response. Today, modernism can still be seen in architecture and design, with prevalent examples being rural retreats that highlight the use of minimalism in their aesthetic of being in contrast with natural surroundings. Overall, modernism in architecture has had a significant impact on architecture, design, and art, and continues to influence these fields today.

References

https://artincontext.org/modern-art/

Artincontext. (2022, March 7). Modern art - an exploration of the 20th-century modernist movement. artincontext.org. Retrieved February 28, 2023, from https://artincontext.org/modern-art/

https://modernism-literature-movement.weebly.com/cubism.html

Cubism. Modernism. (n.d.). Retrieved February 28, 2023, from https://modernism-literature-movement.weebly.com/cubism.html

https://www.tate.org.uk/art/art-terms/f/futurism

Tate. (n.d.). Futurism. Tate. Retrieved February 28, 2023, from https://www.tate.org.uk/art/art-terms/f/futurism

https://www.tate.org.uk/art/art-terms/a/abstract-expressionism#:~:text=Abstract%20expressionism%20is%20the%20term,and%20the%20impression%20of%20spontaneity

Tate. (n.d.). Abstract expressionism. Tate. Retrieved February 28, 2023, from https://www.tate.org.uk/art/art-terms/a/abstract-expressionism#:~:text=Abstract%20expressionism%20is%20the%20term,and%20the%20impression%20of%20spontaneity

https://www.all-about-photo.com/photo-articles/photo-article/524/what-is-the-impact-of-modern-art-on-society

Larson, 2019: All-About-Photo.com, S. L. (2019, August 27). What is the impact of Modern Art on society? All about photo.com: photo contests, photography exhibitions, galleries, photographers, books, schools and venues. Retrieved February 28, 2023, from https://www.all-about-photo.com/photo-articles/photo-article/524/what-is-the-impact-of-modern-art-on-society

https://blogs.chapman.edu/collections/2015/11/30/contemporary-art-vs-modern-art/

Johnson, J. (2015, November 30). Contemporary art vs. modern art - defining. Escalette Permanent Collection of Art at Chapman University. Retrieved February 28, 2023, from https://blogs.chapman.edu/collections/2015/11/30/contemporary-art-vs-modern-art/

https://www.architecture.com/explore-architecture/modernism

Modernism. RIBA. (n.d.). Retrieved February 28, 2023, from https://www.architecture.com/explore-architecture/modernism

https://www.archdaily.com/932659/minimalist-modern-the-architecture-of-rural-retreats#:~:text=Minimalism%20has%20shaped%20architecture%20for,glass%2C%20steel%20and%20reinforced%2-0concrete.

Baldwin, E. (2022, March 5). Minimalist modern: The architecture of rural retreats. ArchDaily. Retrieved February 28, 2023, from https://www.archdaily.com/932659/minimalist-modern-the-architecture-of-rural-retreats#:~:text=Minimalism%20has%20shaped%20architecture%20for,glass%2C%20steel%20and%20reinforced%2-0concrete.

https://www.metmuseum.org/toah/hd/bauh/hd_bauh.htm

Winton, A. G. (1AD, January 1). The Bauhaus, 1919–1933: Essay: The Metropolitan Museum of Art: Heilbrunn timeline of art history. The Met's Heilbrunn Timeline of Art History. Retrieved February 28, 2023, from https://www.metmuseum.org/toah/hd/bauh/hd_bauh.htm

Ola Uduku, Modernist architecture and 'the tropical' in West Africa: The tropical architecture movement in West Africa, 1948–1970, Habitat International,

Volume 30, Issue 3, 2006,
Pages 396-411,
ISSN 0197-3975,
https://doi.org/10.1016/j.habitatint.2004.11.001.

(https://www.sciencedirect.com/science/article/pii/S0197397505000020)

Contemporary Art and Architecture in a Global Context

By Muhammad Farooq

Contemporary art as global context. A critical estimate:

Modern art has changed into a social phenomenon and a means of statement. Comparing it to what we previously knew is pointless since it is dependent on the consequences of globalization, which we are only now beginning to understand and whose magnitude we are still trying to determine (Meyer, R, 2013).

In the next half of the 20th century or the 21st century, contemporary art develops. Artists today operate in a society that is internationally impactful, multi-cultural, and technologically sophisticated. Their art is a spontaneous fusion of elements, processes, emotions, and themes that continues the boundary-questioning that began in the beginning of the 20th century (Smith, T,2009). Dearth of a united and unifying principle, ideology, or "-ism" characterizes contemporary diverse and eclectic art as a whole. Modern art participates in a cultural conversation that concerns broader contextual frames including nationality, family, and cultural identity. Early 21st-century contemporary art is frequently mentioned as if the concept of current art were novel. Nonetheless, all works of art were once contemporary (Young, J. E, 2000). By giving the present his own art history, Richard Meyer liberates it from historical forgetfulness. The "current" is characterized as the state of existence alive for and together with other moments, artists, and objects in Meyer as she analyzes episodes in the exploration, presentation, and interpretation of early 20th century art and visual culture (Meyer, R, 2013). A significant amount of critical work has been put forth in the recent three to four decades to develop a new cultural idea that might go beyond "modern." Each effort was enhanced to the point that it deliberately or unconsciously highlighted key aspects of the modernist cultural paradigm. Weirdly, this was especially true during the most hostile era of modernization criticism. Confusion arises when "contemporary" art refers to works that may date back many years, while "modernism" relates to even older cultural practices (Smith, T, 2009). In the same way, In rapid succession, Terry Smith issued two works that attempted to unravel this complexity. He sees "a worldwide transition from modern to contemporary" as an epochal change. Present art is seismically different from modern and postmodern art, and this transition needs to be explained and comprehended. Contemporary art is not just art that is currently in existence. By providing a historical perspective on the growth of modern art and reconstructing it into structures that reflect its diversity, Smith tries to establish this unmistakable split (Smith, T, 2006). What is modern art, exactly? a description of the major contemporary art trends. Whilst such art might seem radical, it lacks the Avant-"political garde's utopianism and theoretical radicalism." Architects like Frank Gehry, Santiago Calatrava, and Daniel Libeskind easily fit into this type of "spectacularism," as Smith defines it. He believes that every tendency contributes to the "aesthetics of globalization" even if it appears to have little in common. Smith then shifts to his second current, post-colonial art, with which he has been familiar for a while. There aren't any art movements in this place; rather, the art is distinguished by "diversity, identity, and criticism." Smith finds a lower level of counter-institutional activities (ARIs) that is "particular, tiny, and unassuming"; this is likely the level of grassroots, local collectives, and designer ARIs. This level of operations, which frequently go against cultural norms and the global order, tend to be transient and even virtual in character. These differentiators rarely remain stable; rather, they tend to clash or contend with one another more often (Smith, T, 2009). This raises the question, what defines modern art as such? Since contemporary art has always existed, all of the works Smith cites are, by definition, works of art that are currently being created. Is it possible to live forever in modernity? Smith is open about the fact that trying to create something that should diversify and grow enormously is fraught with tension.

The creation of art markets in the Middle East is an important economic undertaking that will "influence Contemporary Art. in the same way, Western auction houses compete with one another in the area. Sotheby's launches a branch in Qatar, whereas Christie's has chosen Dubai. 3 Tadao Ando was hired by Abu Dhabi to build a museum, where the Louvre will send a portion of its holdings . A modern art museum will soon open in Qatar in addition to the Islamic Art Museum, which just opened. As a result, the Middle East will "affect" the global art world. Art museums are an obvious choice, even if they are still a relatively new institution in the region, and as a result, numerous new museums are already under construction. The first "Global Art Forum," which took place in 2008, asked how art "might change the Middle East," but it is a very different question. Modern art poses a risk of conflict with government censorship due to its critical message and public visibility. After 1989, China serves as an illustration of the price that must be paid for a compromise between government politics and the art market. Only the wealthiest investors and private collectors can afford to take the financial risk of owning art, regardless of its purpose. If we exclude Sharja, whose biennial is brilliantly described by Jack Persekian, artistic director of the Sharja Biennial, the Gulf States may adhere. However, they are more liberal values than their Arab neighbors, but their experience with contemporary art is limited (Rendell, J, 2006). But, if we consider the artists themselves, whether they still reside in the area or pursue careers elsewhere, we find a fresh passion. They have access to previously unimaginable opportunities because of the economic possibility, which is strengthened by the global perspective. The success of the entire project rests on providing artists with "independent spaces for gazing and reading," which are innovative in both art and in general societal affairs. The objective is to produce models for use by artists.

World Art

World sculpture and global painting are also used interchangeably. Yet, biosphere art is a time-honored concept that predates modernism and was previously articulated in universal art outside of museums, despite the fact that it was primarily found in Western institutions. It continues to represent humankind's cultural legacy and art from all eras. In truth, it resolved a long-standing conflict between art and ethnographic institutions by making art from any conceivable provenance acceptable as long as it was excluded from modern mainstream art. international regulations governing the preservation of works of art and monuments explicitly recognize their significance. An excellent case study for the current topic of world art is the "School of Global Art Studies," a revolutionary academic organization housed at Norwich's University of East Anglia. As was customary for formalism and universal aesthetics in contemporary art, objects from Africa and Oceania were collected as "art" and shown alongside works of modern art (Andrén, A,1998). John Onians, a professor there, edited his beautiful " Atlas of World Art," which spans from the Stone Age to the Present, in accordance with this idea. The project was also accompanied by a World Art Library. The book "Global Art Studies," whose contributors include both art critics and ethnographers, organizations who for a long time had belonged to separate schools of thought and methodology, documents a comparable programme at Leiden University.

In a sense, the concept of "World art" is composed by a conception of art that is based on modernism's diversity and currently appears a little strange because it connects a Western conception of art with a variety of, frequently ethnic, productions to which the term "art" is arbitrarily applied (Kester, G. H, 2011). Any shape or creation that humans have made is art, according to modernist aesthetics. The best description of world art, which is a kind of visual appropriation of objects as pure form or as evidence of individual creativity on a global level, which is actually a museum in the mind and thus best represents world art, which is also a construct. Ethnographers focused on local goods in a culturally particular manner and so in the most concrete terms; they were never interested in world art. While it is true that terms like "ethnic" or "primitive" raise ethical concerns, they do so for completely different reasons. Sally Price highlights the issue of western art appropriation.

Relationship Between Art and Architecture in Modernism

The clue of integrating fine art and construction has been around since the beginning of the profession, but it acquired fresh importance. Some of today's greatest architects to, demonstrate the close connection in their work (Roberts, D, 2011). It goes without saying that the expectation of a moral and material reconstruction of a post-war world led to the birth of modernity in order to strengthen the sense of community and, by extension, the ties between the city and its residents. In this setting, artistic expression is employed as a tool to mold the emotions of the audience, to whom the marriage of art and architecture can bestow new meaning and provide a setting that conveys a sense of community beyond practicality and technology (Schwarz, D. R, (1997) . Art and architecture are creative fields and the main difference between the two is that architecture, with all of its artistic side, has to function and is built for a specific purpose. For example, if it is a temple, consideration should be given to where and how the idol of God will be placed; where the priest preaches and where the people must enter and where the idols are visible and illuminated. An architect can bring creativity to design, use of different materials, design and lighting design, color and decoration. But all of these variations have limitations and the architect must work within this limited creative realm. Artists, on the other hand, are free to reproduce what they imagine, what is reflected in their works; their scope is infinite, while the architecture is subordinate to the reality of matter. They must seriously consider "load stability, space, materials, light, seasons, heat, water, humidity, and safety, as well as aspects such as serviceability, fitness for purpose, as well as aesthetic factors. All Factors of Reality.

Contemporary and international art and achievement of modernity has encouraged the export of Western art to other parts of the world, where the corresponding desire to join the "developed" countries has laid the foundation. New political and economic leaders who hastened to catch up with the West in the postwar years, after the US had provided as a guide for embracing formerly European modernism, shared and emulated modern as a "project.". Nonetheless, the fundamental issue remained with the concept of "what is art and what is not," as long as non-Western artists were to be excluded due to the hegemonic modernism that was still in place. The only other option to counteract the colonial definition was an excessive nationalism in the representation of modern art.

When abstraction in the 1950s was acknowledged as a worldwide style, or, to use the terminology of the day, a "world language," modern art was defined at the time as modern form in art, even if it could merely mean form without any subject matter. Given this context, the distinction between global and local art is all too clear because the latter no longer insists on form as a primary or independent purpose and lacks any common idiom in terms of style. Instead, modern subject matter and a contemporary performance typically a blend of film, video, and documentary materials are fresh indications of professionalism that set art apart (Frascina, F., Harrison, C., & Paul, D. (Eds.). (1982). As a result, the traditional entrance ticket of formal innovation and purity, as a sign of advanced art, is no longer necessary for membership in the art world. The conscience, ideally viewed as a critical examination of today's most contentious topics, is what really counts. When an artist expresses themselves, originality was previously expected; now, it's a means to stand apart. Will art museums go back in time to provide a context for art, even as that art travels down new, unexpected paths. In the modern era, an institutional framework typically served to define art. In art museums, you might see works of art. Due to artists' calls for a different sort of museum, museums frequently became the focus of an institutional critique. The context was provided by the museum. But the art market does not provide an alternative framework, and institutions have lost their prior authority as a provided setting.

Contemporary art and architecture in a global context

The link between the ideological values of a social or political system and architecture can be easily identified throughout history and it is in fact impossible to consider architecture independently of the influences of the time, which include the social, economic, political and ideological factors of each era. Some historical eras have shown how architectural styles can serve as a means of propagating some national, political and/or social ideals. In his essay 'Towards his critique of architecture ideology' (1969), Tafuri pointed out that 'ideologies have played a dominant role throughout history in certain styles of architecture' in which architects were only 'agents of politics'. Compared to other artistic disciplines, architecture has great potential to exhibit and promote certain ideologies as it easily reaches its recipients and daily life. Values and ideals to free the architectural profession from ties to political ideologies (Kester, G. H, 2011). Avant-garde resistance to the political and ideological specificities of historical styles in art and architecture can be characterized as anarchism, or as an alternative to politics, as Tafuri explains: and the Bauhaus did not hesitate to present itself as a global alternative to politics. cheap. The modernist movement embraced a new alternative ideology that included the promotion of international values and technocratic architectural features, and rejected ornament, historical references, and any form of national or ethnic symbolism (Andrén, A, 1998). In this sense, the 20th century can be seen as the era of architecture's liberation from the influence of political or national ideologies, as well as the era of professional emancipation of architects. Many theorists have noted a strong analogy between contemporary architecture and the International Style, based on the similarities between the processes of globalization of the 21st century and 20th century internationalization, as well as the fundamental importance of technological progress that has dominated both the contemporary, the is the modern architectural Dutch critic Hans Ibe Lings says: "The 90s can be seen as the superlative of the modernist 50s. Internationalization".

Conclusion

Globalization cannot longer be dismissed as a fad or a phantasm in the changing art world. The phrase "global art" still meets with resistance, despite the fact that globalization is the single most important event in today's art scene, even surpassing the introduction of new media art a generation ago. Yet, in the era of "hypermodernity," the "free" movement of markets and media is turned against identity claims by global art, which intensifies antagonism "The absolute newness of the present scenario," says Marc Augé. "While the world's population has now achieved true contemporaneity, the world's variety is always changing. As a result, we must refer to the worlds collectively, realizing that they all interact with one another. Although the planarization of information may have eliminated old borders. The same media make the disparities between the old and new even more obvious. This opposition also holds true for art museums, which continue to be "location specific" in both their architecture and their patronage. They are created to serve as settings for displaying the local condition in the context of international art trade. The universal takes on a local relevance for any listener (Kester, G. H, 2011). In this way, museums continue to serve as emblematic locations and enclaves for a particular culture or a group of people who are adapting to a different culture. The challenge is striking a balance between owning and giving. Even while there may be global sharing, local ownership will always predominate. Global art did not appear overnight or by sheer "chance," but instead after a prolonged incubation period, the results of that which are only now becoming apparent. Its growth is significantly linked to the economic and political shifts that boosted art to the status of a sign of world free trade. When a "new world order" was established, "the art world quickly remade itself (Andrén, A, 1998). Worldwide art events proliferated, and artists from many nations, ethnic groups, and cultures that the West had long overlooked became critically and financially successful. As the cold war came to an end, multicultural art exhibitions began to flourish. The first performances of this kind were seen in 1989 in London and Paris, two towns with a colonial past. One of these was the renowned "Les magiciens de la terre" show by Jean Hubert Martin, which was praised as "the first global exhibition of contemporary art" but also critiqued as the incorrect place to start because it tempted to "exotize Third World artists" (Murphy, M, 2013).Global art frequently defies the claims of art history since it no longer adheres to a larger narrative and challenges modernity's assumption that it is or gives a global model. That two new volumes on world art have chosen to analyze the current status of the art is notable. Julian Stallabrass, whose book is appropriately titled "Art incorporated," addresses the "new world order" in one of his chapters and the effects of our "consumption culture" on contemporary art in another. The title of Charlotte Bydler's book, "The Worldwide Art

World Incorporated," is much more obvious. She actually examines two topics that are uncommon in art criticism (Stallabrass, J, 2020). . They are the evaporation of a popular notion of art and institutional history, correspondingly. The two publications so illustrate that global art has carried on the migration of art from art history.

References

Smith, T. (2009). What is contemporary art?. University of Chicago Press.

Meyer, R. (2013). What was contemporary art?. MIT Press.

Smith, T. (2006). Contemporary art and contemporaneity. Critical Inquiry, 32(4), 681-707.

Meyer, R. What Was Contemporary Art?. Critique d'art, Livres par auteur.

Rendell, J. (2006). Art and architecture: a place between.

Andrén, A. (1998). Between artifacts and texts: historical archaeology in global perspective. Springer Science & Business Media.

Kester, G. H. (2011). The one and the many: Contemporary collaborative art in a global context. Duke University Press.

Young, J. E. (2000). At memory's edge: After-images of the Holocaust in contemporary art and architecture. Yale University Press.

Rendell, J. (2006). Art and architecture: a place between (pp. 1-240). London: IB Tauris.

Roberts, D. (2011). The total work of art in European modernism. In The Total Work of Art in European Modernism. Cornell University Press.

Stallabrass, J. (2020). Contemporary art: a very short introduction (Vol. 146). Oxford University Press, USA.

Murphy, M. (2013). Des Magiciens de la terre, à la globalisation du monde de l'art: retour sur une exposition historique. Critique d'art. Actualité internationale de la littérature critique sur l'art contemporain, (41).

Schwarz, D. R. (1997). Reconfiguring modernism: Explorations in the relationship between modern art and modern literature (p. 241). New York: St. Martin's Press.

Frascina, F., Harrison, C., & Paul, D. (Eds.). (1982). Modern art and modernism: a critical anthology. Sage.

Meyer, R. (2013). What was contemporary art?. MIT Press.

Conclusion

The evolution of art and architecture has been a continuous process, shaped by the cultural, social, and technological changes of each era. This book has provided a comprehensive overview of the major artistic and architectural styles that have emerged over the course of human history. From the grandeur of ancient Greece and Rome to the minimalism of the modernist era, and the postmodern movement's challenge to convention, the book shows how art and architecture have continued to evolve and shape our world in countless ways.

www.ingramcontent.com/pod-product-compliance
Lightning Source LLC
LaVergne TN
LVHW050939080826
845145LV00004B/1324

* 9 7 8 1 7 7 8 8 9 0 2 6 0 *